MASTER EON'S
OFFICIAL GUIDE

GROSSET & DUNLAP
Published by the Penguin Group
Penguin Group (USA) Inc., 375 Hudson Street, New York, New York 10014, USA
Penguin Group (Canada), 90 Eglinton Avenue East, Suite 700, Toronto, Ontario M4P 2Y3, Canada
(a division of Pearson Penguin Canada Inc.)
Penguin Books Ltd., 80 Strand, London WC2R 0RL, England
Penguin Group Ireland, 25 St. Stephen's Green, Dublin 2, Ireland
(a division of Penguin Books Ltd.)
Penguin Group (Australia), 250 Camberwell Road, Camberwell, Victoria 3124, Australia
(a division of Pearson Australia Group Pty. Ltd.)
Penguin Books India Pvt. Ltd., 11 Community Centre, Panchsheel Park, New Delhi—110 017, India
Penguin Group (NZ), 67 Apollo Drive, Rosedale, Auckland 0632, New Zealand
(a division of Pearson New Zealand Ltd.)
Penguin Books (South Africa) (Pty.) Ltd., 24 Sturdee Avenue,
Rosebank, Johannesburg 2196, South Africa

Penguin Books Ltd., Registered Offices: 80 Strand, London WC2R 0RL, England

ISBN 978-0-448-46182-3   10 9 8 7 6 5 4 3 2

MASTER EON'S
OFFICIAL GUIDE

Grosset & Dunlap
An Imprint of Penguin Group (USA) Inc.

CONTENTS

SKYLANDERS:
The Beginning

GREETINGS,
PORTAL MASTER!

Welcome to what may well be the most important book you will ever read . . . even if I do say so myself. Written on its invaluable pages, you will find everything you need to begin your journey with the Skylanders. If they are to stand any chance of defeating the despicable Kaos, they will need your help.

So let me explain where the Skylanders come from and exactly what Skylands is.

WHAT IS SKYLANDS?

Skylands is an ancient world of floating islands in a sea of clouds, filled with wonder, magic, and mystery. This once-magnificent realm had long been protected by the wisest and most powerful beings of all: the Portal Masters.

I was the last Portal Master to have ever lived, and some would say the greatest (not that I'm one to blow my own trumpet!). It was my Skylanders who protected the Core of Light until our darkest day descended upon us . . . literally!

More on Skylands

THE CORE OF LIGHT

The Core of Light was built by the Benevolent Ancients and protected all Skylanders from a mysterious evil known as the Darkness. The Core held a magical power that had enriched Skylands for centuries and kept the Darkness at bay . . . until now!

The Core of Light illuminates the realm of Skylands.

THE DARKNESS

My concern grows as Kaos and the Darkness approach the Core of Light.

No one knows exactly what the Darkness is or where it came from, but we do know it's pretty nasty! Some believe the Benevolent Ancients once took their magic experiments too far and were responsible for letting the Darkness into Skylands. Others say it just sort of appeared, like a cloud or, er, a wasp.

On its own, the Darkness is not effective. It must channel itself through the weak and, in the case of the evil Portal Master Kaos, the idiotic. After the Core of Light was destroyed, my worst fears came true: The Darkness began to spread and Kaos got his cold, unusually small hands on Skylands.

BANISHING THE SKYLANDERS

When Kaos destroyed the Core of Light, a massive explosion erupted across Skylands, propelling the Skylanders away from their world and out into space. They rocketed across the universe, freezing and shrinking into motionless figures until they eventually landed on Earth. It's here that you no doubt discovered them. You'll hopefully also have found a Portal of Power, because without this, your efforts against Kaos will be futile.

EON'S SPIRIT

Hugo and I look on helplessly as the Core of Light is destroyed.

The tiny, frozen Skylanders careen across the universe toward Earth.

During the mighty explosion on Skylands, I was pulled into my own Portal. Not ideal, I know, but there was little I could do to prevent it. Due to this, I no longer appear in my human form. Instead, I am forever locked in the space between realms as a spirit. But do not fear, my young Portal Master. I shall be with you throughout your journey, both in Skylands and within these pages.

You must send your Skylanders back home through the Portal of Power as quickly as you can. There's a crazy bald-headed villain to stop, you know!

Good luck, young Portal Master. I shall be watching!

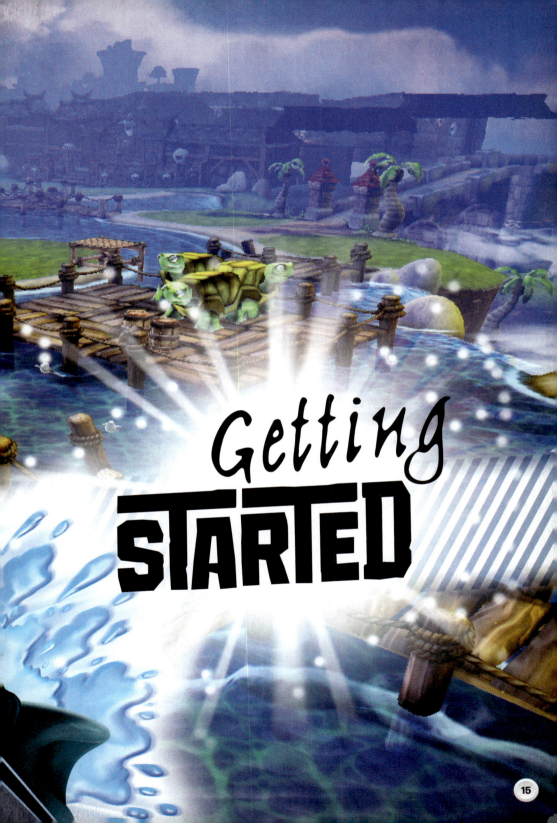

Getting STARTED

GAME STATS

The Skylanders you hold in your hands are deceiving. Although they may look like tiny toys, every Skylander is a living, breathing creature. As you bring them back to life on Skylands, they can run, jump, defend themselves, and battle the enemy. So be careful not to lose them behind the sofa! To see the progress of each Skylander, simply analyze the information within Champion Details.

Keep an eye on your Skylanders' stats as you battle the Darkness. You can increase them by leveling up, completing Cali's heroic challenges, or even by wearing various hats! I'm counting on you to do the best you can.

KEY STATS

 MAX HEALTH
 SPEED
 ARMOR
 CRITICAL HIT
 ELEMENTAL POWER
 HEROICS
 HERO LEVEL

CHAMPION DETAILS

STATS

Max Health	260
Speed	43
Armor	18
Critical Hit	30
Elemental Power	39
Heroics	0
Hero Level	0

Cynder — Undead — Level 1

POWERS MANAGE

Y More Info B Back

ELEMENTs

Every Skylander is strong in one Element. At present, we know of eight Elements that exist in our realm, but there may be more that lie undiscovered. Throughout Skylands, the islands and specific areas within them are stronger in one Element. Some areas even have special Elemental Gates that can only be opened by a Skylander with a matching Element. Be careful which Skylanders you use throughout your journey. If you use the correct Skylander at the right time, then your mission to defeat Kaos will gain serious momentum. If not, you'll let down the entire world. No pressure!

There are eight known Elements.

THE CORE OF LIGHT IS CREATED BY THESE RAW ELEMENTS:

 FIRE

 WATER

 EARTH

 AIR

 LIFE

 UNDEAD

 MAGIC

 TECH

LEVEL UP

Leveling up is where you increase your Skylander by one level until they get to level 10. You can do this by collecting tiny, colored orbs. These will appear once you have defeated an enemy. By collecting these orbs, your Skylanders' experience will increase. This is shown in the yellow bar beneath the health gauge.

WHAT DOES **LEVELING UP** DO?

Each time you move up a level, your Skylander's health points (and chances of survival!) will increase.

EON'S TIPS

Just because you have completed a chapter, it doesn't mean you have to say farewell to it forever. You can replay levels over and over again without even needing to change to a different Skylander!

BUFF UP

Your Skylanders have great powers from the beginning, but you can upgrade these original powers throughout the game.

EON'S TIPS

Watch out for a fairy named Persephone. She opens a shop in the Ruins where your Skylanders can trade their gold coins for upgrades.

INCREASE YOUR STATS

Another way to increase your Skylanders' stats is to complete Cali's Heroic Challenges. They are set against the clock, so you'll need nerves of steel. Look out for her in Chapter 2.

COLLECTIBLE ITEMS

SOUL GEMS

Keep an eye out for these purple gems! Each Soul Gem unlocks an upgrade. Find one of these and race to Persephone as quickly as you can to trade it in!

STORY SCROLLS

Like the Legendary Treasures, every chapter also has a Story Scroll to discover. These are easier to find and well worth reading.

LEGENDARY TREASURES

Every chapter has one Legendary Treasure hidden somewhere. They are sometimes so difficult to discover that even a great Portal Master like myself can struggle to see them!

TREASURE CHEST

Three Treasure Chests are hidden in each chapter of your Skylands adventure. Search, discover, and simply shake to open!

EON'S TIPS Release the gold and gems from the Treasure Chests to boost your bank account.

HATS

In Skylands, a hat isn't just a hat–it's a very important item for defense and attack. Wearing certain hats can increase your speed, strength, and armor. Make it your mission to help your Skylanders track down any hat boxes as they proceed through the islands. When you find one, shake it until the hat appears. The hats can be large, small, funny, and magnificent, but all have an important purpose. Happy hunting!

Hats can be worn by any Skylander, whether they found it (or suit it!) or not.

NAME	LOCATION	STAT BONUS	
Anvil Hat	Shattered Island	+5 Armor	
Beret	Crawling Catacombs	+15 Critical Hit	
Birthday Hat	Perilous Pastures	+2 Critical Hit, +1 Speed	
Bone Head	Cadaverous Crypt	+3 Speed, +7 Elemental Power	
Combat Hat	Battlefield	+15 Elemental Power	
Coonskin Cap	Falling Forest	+10 Critical Hit	
Cowboy Hat	Perilous Pastures	+2 Critical Hit, + 2 Armor	
Crown of Light	Cadaverous Crypt	+15 Armor	
Eye Hat	Crystal Eye Castle	+5 Critical Hit, +5 Elemental Power	
Fancy Hat	Stormy Stronghold	+2 Armor, +1 Speed	
Fez	Stormy Stronghold	+5 Elemental Power	
General's Hat	Goo Factory	+7 Critical Hit, +7 Elemental Power	
Jester Hat	Sky Schooner Docks	+1 Speed, +2 Elemental Power	
Lil Devil	Lava Lakes Railway	+9 Speed	
Miner Hat	Molekin Mine	+7 Armor, +7 Elemental Power	
Moose Hat	Treetop Terrace	+5 Armor, +2 Speed	
Napoleon Hat	Leviathan Lagoon	+5 Armor, +5 Elemental Power	
Pan Hat	Shattered Island	+2 Armor, +2 Elemental Power	
Plunger Head	Oilspill Island	+2 Critical Hit, +2 Elemental Power	
Propeller Cap	Sky Schooner Docks	+3 Speed	
Rocker Hair	Creepy Citadel	+7 Critical Hit, +3 Elemental Power	
Rocket Hat	Troll Warehouse	+6 Speed	
Spiked Hat	Goo Factory	+7 Critical Hit, +7 Armor	
Spy Gear	Troll Warehouse	+5 Critical Hit, +2 Speed	
Tiki Hat	Dark Water Cove	+10 Elemental Power	
Top Hat	Stonetown	+5 Critical Hit, +5 Armor	
Trojan Helmet	Crystal Eye Castle	+10 Armor	
Tropical Turban	Dark Water Cove	+2 Speed, +5 Elemental Power	
Unicorn Hat	Quicksilver Vault	+12 Critical Hit, +12 Armor	
Viking Helmet	Shattered Island	+5 Critical Hit	
Wabbit Ears	Lair of Kaos	+12 Armor, +5 Speed	

ADVENTURE PACK HATS

Chef Hat	Darklight Crypt	+10 Critical Hit, +10 Elemental Power	
Cossack Hat	Empire of Ice	+10 Elemental Power	
Pirate Doo Rag	Pirate Seas	+4 Speed	
Pirate Hat	Pirate Seas	+20 Critical Hit	
Pumpkin Hat	Darklight Crypt	+10 Armor	
Royal Crown	Dragon's Peak	+10 Critical Hit	
Santa Hat	Empire of Ice	+20 Armor	
Winged Hat	Dragon's Peak	+12 Speed	

CONSOLE-SPECIFIC ADVENTURE PACK HATS

Bowler Hat	Perilous Pastures	+2 Critical Hit, + 2 Armor	PC/Mac
Straw Hat	Perilous Pastures	+2 Critical Hit, + 2 Armor	Playstation 3
Happy Birthday!	Perilous Pastures	+2 Critical Hit, + 2 Armor	Nintendo Wii

WINGED SAPPHIRES

WHAT ARE THEY?

Winged Sapphires are great for acquiring upgrade discounts from Persephone.

WHAT DO THEY LOOK LIKE?

They are floating blue gems with wings, like an odd, shiny butterfly.

WHERE ARE THEY?

Winged Sapphires are found in the Ruins. There are not many to find, so keep an eye out for them!

EON'S TIPS

The first Winged Sapphire appears in the Ruins after you make it through Sky Schooner Docks. Try to find it before venturing on.

ACCOLADES EXPLAINED

As a new Portal Master, you should familiarize yourself with these accolades. If you are to follow in my footsteps and become something of a legend, you should aim to gain as many of them as you can. Here's a list of how you can earn them . . .

ACCOLADE	COLLECTION REQUIREMENTS
1 Captain	At least one non-Starter Pack Skylander
2 Ambassador	One Skylander of each Element
3 Sergeant Major	At least eight different Skylanders
4 Commander	At least twelve different Skylanders
5 General	At least sixteen different Skylanders
6 Field Marshall	At least twenty-four different Skylanders
7 Master of Skylands	All thirty-two Skylanders
8 Student of Thought	At least ten Story Scrolls
9 Chief Scholar	All the Story Scrolls
10 Seeker Adept	At least ten Legendary Treasures
11 Treasure Hunter	All twenty-six Legendary Treasures
12 Power Excavator	Soul Gems for each of the three Starter Pack Skylanders
13 Soul Warden	All thirty-two Skylanders' Soul Gems
14 Fashion Elite	At least ten hats
15 Wardrobe Saint	All hats throughout Skylands
16 Elite Agent	A Skylander completes the thirty-two Heroic Challenges
17 Savior of Skylands	Restore the Core of Light and defeat Kaos
18 Skylander Superstar	Earn a three-star ranking on all Adventure Chapters
19 Grand Admiral	Earn all Portal Master accolades

BATTLE
Mode

BATTLE MODE EXPLAINED

As my Skylanders have only recently landed on Earth, you may wish to test your skills as a new Portal Master before sending them into battle.

Here you can summon fellow Portal Masters on Earth to duel against you. As I believe they say on your planet, practice makes perfect!

BATTLE MODE	AIM
Arena Rumble	Reduce your opponent's health to zero!
Sky Goals	Get the electric ball in the goal
SkyGem Master	Who can collect the five gems the quickest?

THE **ARENAS**
CYCLOPS SQUARE
MUSHROOM GROVE
AQUEDUCT
TROLL FACTORY

Pick a battle location, choose your ultimate Skylander, and let the battle begin!

In a Battle Mode head-to-head there's nowhere for a Portal Master to hide!

FAIR FIGHT

You can even out a battle between two Skylanders by going into this option and setting it to "Yes." Some Portal Masters are not all they seem and may have purposely leveled up their Skylanders by battling against poor opponents. To make the battle fair, always select this option.

There are other options available for creating different battle features, too. For example, you can have power-ups, food, and pesky hazards pop up in the arena.

Flameslinger   Voodood

BATTLE MODE ARENAS

CYCLOPS SQUARE

This is a great arena to challenge not only other Portal Masters but also your own agility and skill. Cyclops Square is littered with five bounce pads and three teleport pads for those swift escapes and stealthy attacks, but it also plays host to its own dangers. Beware of staying still for too long on the hole-riddled floor as spears have a nasty tendency to thrust at you from underneath. Ouch!

MUSHROOM GROVE

What a quiet and delicate place for a Portal Master battle. There are no unforeseen dangers lurking here to damage your Skylanders. The only harm that can be inflicted upon them is from the opposition, so this really is a solid test of skill. Here you will find three bounce pads, two teleporters, and lots of lush green grass. It might even be worth agreeing to a "time out" with your challenger so your Skylanders can bask in the sun!

AQUEDUCT

There's very little chance of escaping a good sparring partner in here. The Aqueduct has no teleporters, so you can't make that swift getaway or sneak up on your opponent unsuspectingly. There are, however, three bounce pads, so you can leap from one level to the next to escape. Watch out for the Hazard Activators. If either one is activated, the Aqueduct fills with water. Use the bounce pads to jump to safety or use a Water Skylander as the rising water will not harm them at all. In fact, they'll quite like it!

TROLL FACTORY

This is certainly the most colorful of the Battle Arenas and you can count the number of bounce pads on one hand—assuming you have six fingers! As with the Aqueduct arena, there are no teleporters, but there are two conveyor belts that carry the Skylanders up to the top of the arena. There are two hazards in here and both are flame jets. You will suffer extreme health damage if you're caught in their flames, so steer clear. Not even Skylanders from the Fire Element are immune!

 BOUNCE PAD   **HAZARD ACTIVATORS**   **SKY GOAL**   **TELEPORTER**   **TELEPORTER DESTINATION**

UNLOCKABLE BATTLE MODE ARENAS

CUBE DUNGEON

Jumping cubes . . . literally! This arena has two main hazards—the opponent and the cube that bounces around the dungeon with the full intention of striking a Skylander whenever possible. Watch out for this cube of danger–if it hits your Skylander you will lose 20 Health points.

This arena is unlocked with the Dragon's Peak Adventure Pack.

ICICLE ISLE

If you try to alter the direction of your Skylander while it's on the ice you'll realize it's almost impossible. This is not an arena for the fainthearted. It's cold and icy in here, and only true Portal Masters who wish to showcase their talent should attempt this arena. Good luck!

This arena is unlocked with the Empire of Ice Adventure Pack.

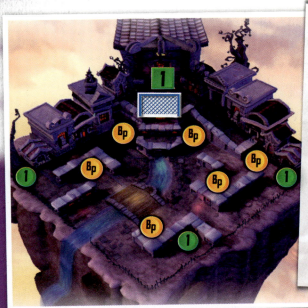

THE NECROPOLIS

If you're a Portal Master who's up for a blast then this could be the arena for you! There's a cannon on the bridge in this arena but unfortunately it can't be angled or turned. It fires at a fixed point, so you'll have to choose your timing well if you want to hit your opponent's Skylander.

This arena is unlocked with the Darklight Crypts Adventure Pack.

PIRATE GROTTO

Pirate Grotto has two Hazard Activators at either end of the arena. When these are activated, they call in a naval bombardment from afar. Yellow crosshairs will swiftly appear on the floor of the arena. Make sure you step right into them . . . if you want to get hit that is!

This arena is unlocked with the Pirate Seas Adventure Pack.

BOUNCE PAD	**HAZARD ACTIVATORS**	**SKY GOAL**	**TELEPORTER**	**TELEPORTER DESTINATION**

Meet the SKYLANDERS

MASTER EON
"THE GREATEST PORTAL MASTER EVER!"

This is me in my spirit form, which I've been in since the Core of Light exploded. It can be quite a talking point at parties.

PERSONALITY FILE

CARING AND KIND
GENEROUS
PROTECTIVE
GREATEST PORTAL MASTER

Skylands was a glorious place before the Darkness struck. Just look at it!

As I am now a spirit and can no longer control the Skylanders myself, I need your help to send them back home where they can use their powers to fight the Darkness that the mean, nasty, and downright irritating Kaos has brought upon Skylands.

Magic flows through everything in Skylands, whether Kaos likes it or not!

Meet the Skylanders

ELEMENT
MAGIC
SKYLANDER

Spyro is one of my strongest leaders and is dedicated to scorching the forces of darkness.

SPYRO
"ALL FIRED UP!"

STARTING STATS

MAX HEALTH	280
SPEED	50
ARMOR	18
CRITICAL HIT	30
ELEMENTAL POWER	25

PERSONALITY FILE

STRONG-WILLED
YOUNG AT HEART
FOUNTAIN OF KNOWLEDGE
VALIANT LEADER

POWERS & UPGRADES

ACTION BUTTON

Flameball–Goodness gracious! Great balls of fire

ATTACK BUTTON

Charge–Does just that. Charge!!

POWER UPGRADES

500 GOLD COINS

Long Range Raze–Fires long range fireballs

700 GOLD COINS

Spyro's Flight–Spyro takes to the skies

900 GOLD COINS

Sprint Charge–Faster charge!!

1200 GOLD COINS

Triple Flameballs–Projects triple fireballs for triple the fun

"CHOOSE YOUR PATH" UPGRADES

PATH 1: SHEEP BURNER SPYRO
Choose this path to increase Spyro's fire-breathing options.

1700 GOLD COINS

Fire Shield–Creates a fire shield while using his fireball attack mode

2200 GOLD COINS

Exploding Fireblast–Creates an exploding fireball to take out multiple enemies

3000 GOLD COINS

The Daybringer Flame–Gives the option to build a massive flame attack. Scorching!

PATH 2: BLITZ SPYRO
Choose this path to increase Spyro's charging abilities.

1700 GOLD COINS

Stun Charge–Stuns enemies when they are hit

2200 GOLD COINS

Comet Dash–Sets Spyro's horns alight to inflict some extra damage

3000 GOLD COINS

Ibex's Wrath Charge–Builds up speed and an increased fiery horn power

TRIGGER HAPPY

"NO GOLD, NO GLORY!"

ELEMENT
TECH
SKYLANDER

I tracked down Trigger Happy after hearing of his noble deeds across the villages of Skylands.

STARTING STATS	
MAX HEALTH	200
SPEED	50
ARMOR	30
CRITICAL HIT	50
ELEMENTAL POWER	25

PERSONALITY FILE

INSANE LAUGHTER
QUICK TRIGGERED
GOLD LOVER
FAST AND FURIOUS

POWERS & UPGRADES

ACTION BUTTON

Golden Pistols–Shoots multiple gold coins for a cash bonanza

ATTACK BUTTON

Lob Golden Safe–Throws golden safes (or not-so-safes) at the enemy

POWER UPGRADES

500 GOLD COINS

Golden Super Charge–Extra-powered coin bullets. Ka-ching!

700 GOLD COINS

Pot O' Gold–Throws a pot of gold

900 GOLD COINS

Golden Mega Charge–Adds even more power to the revolvers

1200 GOLD COINS

Golden Machine Gun–Swaps revolvers for a machine gun

"CHOOSE YOUR PATH" UPGRADES

PATH 1: GOLDEN FRENZY
If you choose this path, you will increase Trigger Happy's Golden Gun attack options.

1700 GOLD COINS

Happiness Is a Golden Gun–Golden Gun causes increased fire damage

2200 GOLD COINS

Bouncing Bullets–Coin bullets deflect off walls

3000 GOLD COINS

Golden Yamato Blast–Increases gun charge to inflict damage

PATH 2: GOLDEN MONEY BAGS
Choose this path to increase Trigger Happy's throwing skills.

1700 GOLD COINS

Just Throwing Money Away–Throw the Pot O' Gold farther

2200 GOLD COINS

Coinsplosion–Pot O' Gold explodes to release coins

3000 GOLD COINS

Heads or Tails–Toss a coin to do extra damage. If it lands heads up, then ka-boom!

ELEMENT
WATER
SKYLANDER

GILL GRUNT

"FEAR THE FISH!"

I encouraged Gill Grunt to become a Skylander after he proved his reputation as a true warrior.

STARTING STATS

MAX HEALTH	270
SPEED	35
ARMOR	6
CRITICAL HIT	50
ELEMENTAL POWER	25

PERSONALITY FILE

GREAT WARRIOR
PROTECTIVE INSTINCTS
BIG HEART
DETERMINED

POWERS & UPGRADES

ACTION BUTTON

Harpoon Gun–Fires fishy harpoons

ATTACK BUTTON

Power Hose–Sprays water

POWER UPGRADES

500 GOLD COINS

500

Thruster Flight–Briefly becomes a flying fish

700 GOLD COINS

700

High Pressue Power Hose–Wet and wild!

900 GOLD COINS

900

Harpoon Repeater–Faster harpoon reloading

1200 GOLD COINS

1200

Water Jetpack–Longer sustained flight

"CHOOSE YOUR PATH" UPGRADES

PATH 1: HARPOONER
If you choose this path, you will increase Gill Grunt's harpoon attack options.

1700 GOLD COINS

1700

Quadent Harpoons–Fire four-pronged harpoons

2200 GOLD COINS

2200

Piercing Harpoons–These harpoons continue to travel straight through your enemies

3000 GOLD COINS

3000

Tripleshot Harpoons–Fire three harpoons at once!

PATH 2: WATER WEAVER
If you choose this path, you will increase Gill Grunt's hose and jet pack options.

1700 GOLD COINS

1700

Reserve Water Tank–Hoses and jet packs sustain their water levels

2200 GOLD COINS

2200

Boiling Water Hose–Power Hose creates extra damage

3000 GOLD COINS

3000

Neptune Gun–Woah! This launches exploding creatures!

ELEMENT
FIRE
SKYLANDER

This brave and selfless knight could not escape my attention as a potential Skylander.

IGNITOR
"SLASH AND BURN!"

STARTING STATS	
MAX HEALTH	240
SPEED	43
ARMOR	12
CRITICAL HIT	40
ELEMENTAL POWER	25

PERSONALITY FILE

SELF-SACRIFICING
BRAVE
HEROIC
RIGHTEOUS

POWERS & UPGRADES

STARTING POWERS

ACTION BUTTON

Flame Blade–Swings flaming sword

ATTACK BUTTON

Flame Form Mortar–Fires flames at enemies

POWER UPGRADES

500 GOLD COINS

Scorching Blade–More powerful flaming sword. Burn, baby, burn!

700 GOLD COINS

Flame Form–Controlled flame launching

900 GOLD COINS

Mega Slam–Launch mega flames

1200 GOLD COINS

Fire and Brimstome–Ultra mega flames!

"CHOOSE YOUR PATH" UPGRADES

PATH 1: SOUL OF THE FLAME
If you choose this path, you will increase Ignitor's flame form abilities.

1700 GOLD COINS

Dances with Fire–Superfast flame

2200 GOLD COINS

Incinerate–Create a mega fire explosion

3000 GOLD COINS

Fire Form Salvo–Fire triple flames

PATH 2: BLADEMASTER
If you choose this path, you will increase Ignitor's Flame Blade skills.

1700 GOLD COINS

Order of the Burning Blade–Fire a burst of flames

2200 GOLD COINS

Double Mega Slam–Perform a mega axe attack

3000 GOLD COINS

Inferno Blade–Increase sword size from sublime to ridiculous

ERUPTOR

"BORN TO BURN!"

There's no doubt that Eruptor is the Skylander with the most fire in his belly.

STARTING STATS	
MAX HEALTH	290
SPEED	35
ARMOR	18
CRITICAL HIT	30
ELEMENTAL POWER	25

PERSONALITY FILE

HOTHEADED
BAD TEMPERED
CONTROLLED ANGER
PRONE TO BURPING

POWERS & UPGRADES

STARTING POWERS

ACTION BUTTON

Lava Lob–Hurls lava at the enemy

ATTACK BUTTON

Eruption–That molten lava goes everywhere

POWER UPGRADES

500 GOLD COINS

Big Blob Lava Throw–It's like a Lava Lob, but bigger!

700 GOLD COINS

Fiery Remains–Lava Lobs leave flames in their wake

900 GOLD COINS

Eruption-Flying Tephra–Flying lava balls mixed with an Eruption

1200 GOLD COINS

Magma Ball–It's Magma ball spitting time!

"CHOOSE YOUR PATH" UPGRADES

PATH 1: MAGMANTOR
If you choose this path, you will increase Eruptor's Lava Blob and Magma Ball throwing skills.

1700 GOLD COINS

Heavy Duty Plasma–Bouncing Lava Blobs . . . literally!

2200 GOLD COINS

Lava Blob Bomb–These blobs explode!

3000 GOLD COINS

Beast of Conflagration–Blobs morph into fierce and fiery beasts

PATH 2: VOLCANOR
If you choose this path, you will increase Eruptor's erupt-ability!

1700 GOLD COINS

Quick Eruption–Superspeed Eruption attacks

2200 GOLD COINS

Pyroxysmal Super Eruption–Mega Eruption attack

3000 GOLD COINS

Revenge of Prometheus–Creates mini volcanoes

ELEMENT
EARTH
SKYLANDER

PRISM BREAK

"THE BEAM IS SUPREME!"

I'll always be grateful to the miners who rediscovered this rock golem and freed him from his hundred-year slumber.

STARTING STATS	
MAX HEALTH	290
SPEED	35
ARMOR	18
CRITICAL HIT	30
ELEMENTAL POWER	25

PERSONALITY FILE

RUTHLESS
POWERFUL
LUMBERING
FEROCIOUS

POWERS & UPGRADES

STARTING POWERS

ACTION BUTTON

Energy Beam–Treats enemies to a beam feast!

ATTACK BUTTON

Summon Crystal Shard–Brings crystal shard into play

POWER UPGRADES

500 GOLD COINS

Super Crystal Shard–Increase crystal shard damage

700 GOLD COINS

Crystal Eruption–Engulfs Prism Break in spiky shards

900 GOLD COINS

Emerald Energy Beam–Inflicts extra damage

1200 GOLD COINS

Chained Refractions–Splits energy beams even more

"CHOOSE YOUR PATH" UPGRADES

PATH 1: CRYSTALEER
If you choose this path, Prism Break's ability to defend himself will increase.

1700 GOLD COINS

Massive Crystal Eruption–Increases damage on an even wider scale

2200 GOLD COINS

Triple Crystal Shard–Creates three shards at the same time

3000 GOLD COINS

Crystalline Armor–Prism Break armors up. Even more than usual, that is!

PATH 2: PRISMANCER
If you choose this path, you will increase Prism Break's energy beam attack options.

1700 GOLD COINS

Golden Diamond Energy Beam–A change of color and extra power

2200 GOLD COINS

Triple Refracted Beam–Three beams multiply the damage

3000 GOLD COINS

Focused Energy–Blasts beams even further

STUMP SMASH

"DROP THE HAMMER!"

Stump Smash came to me after ridding a forest of nasty trolls and saving his fellow trees from becoming kindling.

STARTING STATS	
MAX HEALTH	340
SPEED	43
ARMOR	30
CRITICAL HIT	20
ELEMENTAL POWER	25

PERSONALITY FILE

PROTECTIVE
DO-GOODER
VENGEFUL
TROLL SMASHER!

POWERS & UPGRADES

STARTING POWERS

ACTION BUTTON

Pulverize–Look out–it's smash time!

ATTACK BUTTON

When Acorns Attack–Dish out tree-normous justice

POWER UPGRADES

500 GOLD COINS

500

Petrified Pummel–Increases Stumpfist power

700 GOLD COINS

700

Spiny Acorns–Spit spiny acorns at foes

900 GOLD COINS

900

Meganut–Here we go! It's prickly Meganut time!

1200 GOLD COINS

1200

Thornbark–Generate spiky thorns for attack

PATH 1: SMASH 'N' BASH
Choose this path to add extra power to Stump Smash's Stumpfist assaults.

1700 GOLD COINS

1700

Stump Crusher Combos–Stumpfists increase his rage to mega power

2200 GOLD COINS

2200

Acorn Croquet–Sends Meganut toward your enemy

3000 GOLD COINS

3000

Smash Meganut–Creates a Meganut explosion

PATH 2: NUT CRAFTER
If you choose this path, you'll increase Stump's Acorn and Meganut options.

1700 GOLD COINS

1700

Pollen Plume–Make it a jungle out there!

2200 GOLD COINS

2200

Meganut Propagation–Meganuts burst into acorns

3000 GOLD COINS

3000

Double Nut–It's double acorn spitting time!

"CHOOSE YOUR PATH" UPGRADES

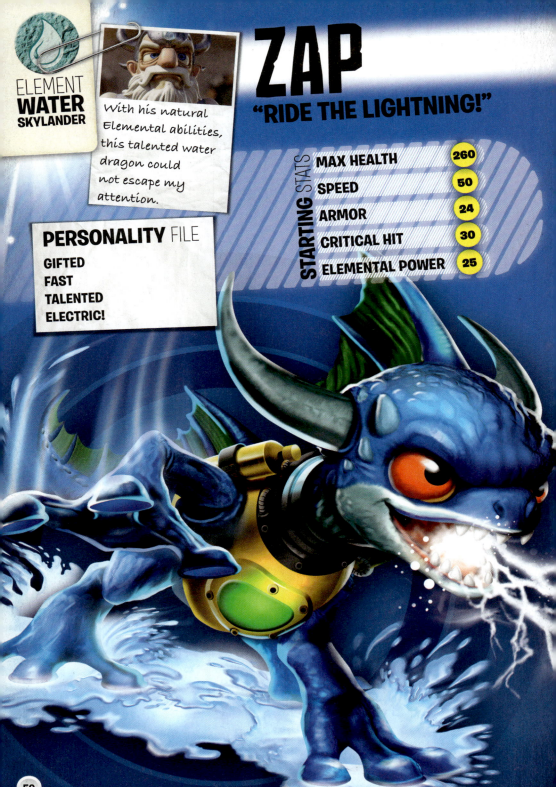

With his natural Elemental abilities, this talented water dragon could not escape my attention.

ZAP
"RIDE THE LIGHTNING!"

STARTING STATS	
MAX HEALTH	260
SPEED	50
ARMOR	24
CRITICAL HIT	30
ELEMENTAL POWER	25

PERSONALITY FILE

GIFTED
FAST
TALENTED
ELECTRIC!

POWERS & UPGRADES

STARTING POWERS

ACTION BUTTON

Lightning Breath–Spits a bolt of yellow electricity

ATTACK BUTTON

Sea Slime Slide–Moves on Sea Slime and glues foes to the spot

POWER UPGRADES

500 GOLD COINS

Electro-Slime–Shoot a stream of slime and electrify it

700 GOLD COINS

Stay a While–Give your Sea Slime an enduring current

900 GOLD COINS

Megavolt–It's a lightning bolt for increased damage

1200 GOLD COINS

Wave Rider–Eradicate enemies with a huge wave

"CHOOSE YOUR PATH" UPGRADES

PATH 1: TESLA DRAGON
If you choose this path, you'll increase Zap's lightning and wave power.

1700 GOLD COINS

Lightning Strikes Twice–Creates deflecting and bouncing lightning bolts

2200 GOLD COINS

Electric Wave–It's a mammoth wave attack!

3000 GOLD COINS

Tesla Storm–Open wide and let out a colossal bolt of lightning

PATH 2: SLIME SERPENT
If you choose this path, you will increase Zap's Sea Slime options.

1700 GOLD COINS

Strength in Numbers–Creates extra Sea Slime

2200 GOLD COINS

Charged with Punishment–Electrifies all the Sea Slime

3000 GOLD COINS

More Electro'd Slime–More damage to enemies stuck in electrified Sea Slime

FLAMESLINGER

"LET THE FLAMES BEGIN!"

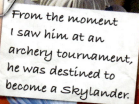

From the moment I saw him at an archery tournament, he was destined to become a Skylander.

STARTING STATS	
MAX HEALTH	250
SPEED	50
ARMOR	24
CRITICAL HIT	40
ELEMENTAL POWER	25

PERSONALITY FILE

COMMITTED
MYSTICAL VISION
INCREDIBLE SPEED
SELFLESS

POWERS & UPGRADES

ACTION BUTTON

Fire Arrow–Shoot a flaming arrow at your enemies

ATTACK BUTTON

Flame Dash–Sprint forward leaving a blazing trail behind

POWER UPGRADES

500 GOLD COINS

Searing Arrows–Flaming arrows cause extra damage

700 GOLD COINS

Column of Fire–Sprint in a circle to create a flaming column

900 GOLD COINS

Volley Shot–Shoot blazing arrow rain at your foes

1200 GOLD COINS

Hyper Shot–Increases the speed of the flaming arrows

"CHOOSE YOUR PATH" UPGRADES

PATH 1: MARKSMAN

Choose this path to give Flameslinger's Fire Arrow options a boost.

1700 GOLD COINS

Hellfire Arrows–Fiery arrows point one way: toward pain!

2200 GOLD COINS

Explosive Arrows–Watch those arrows explode in a stream of fire

3000 GOLD COINS

Triple Shot Arrows–Unleash three blazing arrows at once and make Robin Hood look like an amateur

PATH 2: PYROMANCER

If you choose this path, Flameslinger's ability to cause vast fires will increase.

1700 GOLD COINS

Napalm Tipped Arrows–Arrows leave a burning trail–and enemies weeping. Waaah!

2200 GOLD COINS

Inferno Blast–Charge up a blazing blast and unleash it to destroy anything in its path

3000 GOLD COINS

Supernova–Sprint in a circle with the Flame Dash and leave a fire that will spread quickly

ELEMENT
UNDEAD
SKYLANDER

CHOP CHOP
"SLICE AND DICE!"

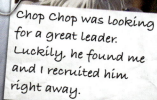

Chop Chop was looking for a great leader. Luckily, he found me and I recruited him right away.

PERSONALITY FILE

WARRIOR
DRIVEN
RELENTLESS
FOLLOWS ORDERS

POWERS & UPGRADES

STARTING POWERS

ACTION BUTTON

Arkeyan Blade–Slashing ancient blade

ATTACK BUTTON

Arkeyan Shield–For a mighty defense

POWER UPGRADES

500 GOLD COINS

Spiked Shield Bash–Jabs the shield at the enemy

700 GOLD COINS

Vampiric Aura–Causes extra damage and restores health

900 GOLD COINS

Shield Spartan–Quicker speed and more blocks

1200 GOLD COINS

Bone Brambler–Attack the enemy with sharp bone brambles

"CHOOSE YOUR PATH" UPGRADES

PATH 1: VAMPIRIC WARRIOR
If you choose this path, you will create better sword attack options.

1700 GOLD COINS

Arkeyan Combat Master– Creates a spinning cyclone attack

2200 GOLD COINS

Arkeyan Vorpal Blade–Slice and dice in mega style for increased damage

3000 GOLD COINS

Demon Blade of the Underworld– Every bit as bad as it sounds

PATH 2: UNDEAD DEFENDER
Choose this path to provide Chop Chop with extra defensive options.

1700 GOLD COINS

Arkeyan Spectral Shield– Absorb attacks and return the power with extra fury

2200 GOLD COINS

Shield Stun Bash–Spiked shield stuns attackers

3000 GOLD COINS

Demon Shield of the Shadows– Shield absorbs damage and sends it back, with interest!

DARK SPYRO

"LIGHTS OUT!"

Dark Spyro can absorb dark magic and control it to unleash even more devastating fire attacks.

STARTING STATS	
MAX HEALTH	280
SPEED	50
ARMOR	18
CRITICAL HIT	30
ELEMENTAL POWER	25

PERSONALITY FILE

VULNERABLE
LOVES FIRE
BRAVE
GREAT IN BATTLE

POWERS & UPGRADES

STARTING POWERS

ACTION BUTTON

Flameball–Unleash the death breath!

ATTACK BUTTON

Charge–Sends villains running for their lives

POWER UPGRADES

500 GOLD COINS

500

Long Range Raze–Leaves enemies extracrispy

700 GOLD COINS

700

Spyro's Flight–Dark Spyro goes up, up and away

900 GOLD COINS

900

Sprint Charge–Superfast charging ability

1200 GOLD COINS

1200

Triple Flameballs–Three's a charm . . . or should that be "harm"?

"CHOOSE YOUR PATH" UPGRADES

PATH 1: SHEEP BURNER SPYRO

Choose this path for extra fire-breathing attack options.

1700 GOLD COINS

1700

Fire Shield–Disobeys virtually all recognized fire safety laws–and does it in style!

2200 GOLD COINS

2200

Exploding Fireblast–For that extralarge fireball

3000 GOLD COINS

3000

The Daybringer Flame–An extra flame attack for a sizzling good time

---

PATH 2: BLITZ SPYRO

If you choose this path, you will increase Dark Spyro's charging abilities.

1700 GOLD COINS

1700

Stun Charge–Burn 'n' stun

2200 GOLD COINS

2200

Comet Dash–Turn Dark Spyro into a hothead

3000 GOLD COINS

3000

Ibex's Wrath Charge–You do not want to find yourself on the end of these horns

STEALTH ELF

"SILENT BUT DEADLY!"

Stealth Elf was introduced to me and I immediately saw that her skills would make her an ideal Skylander.

STARTING STATS

MAX HEALTH	270
SPEED	50
ARMOR	12
CRITICAL HIT	50
ELEMENTAL POWER	25

PERSONALITY FILE

AGILE AND NIMBLE
SKILLED BEYOND HER YEARS
FAST AND SPEEDY
PROTECTOR

POWERS & UPGRADES

ACTION BUTTON

Blade Slash–Sharp blades will slice the enemy

ATTACK BUTTON

Stealthier Decoy–Vanish and leave behind a decoy

POWER UPGRADES

500 GOLD COINS

Straw Pook Scarecrow–A scarecrow distracts the enemy (and any passing crows)

700 GOLD COINS

Dragonfang Dagger–Sharp blades inflict extra damage

900 GOLD COINS

Sturdy Scarecrow–Scarecrows last longer and are even harder to destroy

1200 GOLD COINS

Arboreal Acrobatics–Part attack, part dance move!

"CHOOSE YOUR PATH" UPGRADES

PATH 1: POOK BLADE SAINT
Choose this path to increase Stealth Elf's blade attack options.

1700 GOLD COINS

Elf Jitsu–Woah! This creates nasty poisonous spores

2200 GOLD COINS

Elven Sunblade–Sharp blades do increased damage

3000 GOLD COINS

Shadowsbane Blade Dance–Mysterious and magical blades join the fight

PATH 2: FOREST NINJA
If you choose this path, you will enhance Stealth Elf's scarecrow skills.

1700 GOLD COINS

Scare-crio Trio–Triple scarecrows are left behind as decoys

2200 GOLD COINS

Scarecrow Booby Trap–These scarecrows have a tendency to explode!

3000 GOLD COINS

Scarecrow Spin Slicer–Scarecrow's axes do increased damage to pesky foes

VOODOOD

"AXE FIRST, QUESTIONS LATER!"

All alone, Voodood had vowed to protect others. That's as good a start as any!

STARTING STATS

MAX HEALTH	290
SPEED	35
ARMOR	12
CRITICAL HIT	30
ELEMENTAL POWER	25

PERSONALITY FILE

BRAVE
TIRELESS
MAGICAL
DETERMINED

POWERS & UPGRADES

STARTING POWERS

ACTION BUTTON

Axe Reaver-Wields the legendary axe

ATTACK BUTTON

Zipline Axe-Launch the axe blade to be reeled in

POWER UPGRADES

500 GOLD COINS

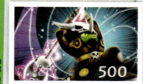

Magical Tripwire Bomb-A tripwire that collapses on the enemy

700 GOLD COINS

Weighted Axe-Cause extra pain with this mega axe attack

900 GOLD COINS

Tripwire Reserves-Create double tripwires

1200 GOLD COINS

Extended Blade-The Zipline Axe is better and faster

"CHOOSE YOUR PATH" UPGRADES

PATH 1: ELEMENTALIST
If you choose this path, you will increase Voodood's magical abilities.

1700 GOLD COINS

Roadblock Tripwire-Extended tripwires cause extra damage

2200 GOLD COINS

Electric Feedback-Create a magical aura of energy to defeat all nearby enemies

3000 GOLD COINS

Electro Axe-The axe strike destroys all nearby foes

PATH 2: CONJUROR
If you choose this path, you will improve Voodood's axe-wielding skills.

1700 GOLD COINS

Shaman Style-Look out! It's the axe spinning combo attack

2200 GOLD COINS

Legendary Blade-It's even bigger and better than any axe attack so far

3000 GOLD COINS

Hyperwire-It's a mega fast Zipline Axe. Whee!

ELEMENT
TECH
SKYLANDER

He was plummeting through the sky when I saved him and offered him a new, non-plummet-based way of life.

BASH
"ROCK-N-ROLL!"

STARTING STATS		
MAX HEALTH		310
SPEED		35
ARMOR		12
CRITICAL HIT		20
ELEMENTAL POWER		25

PERSONALITY FILE

ROLLING EXPERT
COURAGEOUS
WILLFUL
DETERMINED

POWERS & UPGRADES

STARTING POWERS

ACTION BUTTON

Tail Swipe-Tail swipes to destroy enemies at 360 degrees

ATTACK BUTTON

Rock and Roll-Bowls over the enemies in a dragony ball

POWER UPGRADES

500 GOLD COINS

Tennis Tail-Knock back incoming enemy objects with the tail

700 GOLD COINS

Iron Tail-Inflict mega damage with this tail swipe. Boom!

900 GOLD COINS

Summoning Stone Projection-Launch rocks from a rock wall

1200 GOLD COINS

Double Roll-Double duration roll attack

PATH 1: GRANITE DRAGON

If you choose this path, you will increase Bash's tail swipe attack.

"CHOOSE YOUR PATH" UPGRADES

1700 GOLD COINS

Mace Destruction-Tail mace is ready to unleash more mayhem

2200 GOLD COINS

Summoning Stone Uppercut-Mega stone fist is created to do some damage

3000 GOLD COINS

Gaia Hammer-A charged tail swipe will do more damage than ever before

PATH 2: PULVER DRAGON

Choose this path to build up Bash's roll attack.

1700 GOLD COINS

Pulver Roll-Look out! Mega roll coming through!

2200 GOLD COINS

Earthen Force Roll-Crushes the enemy in a single roll

3000 GOLD COINS

Continental Boulder-Increases size and speed of the roll attack

SONIC BOOM

"FULL SCREAM AHEAD!"

ELEMENT
AIR
SKYLANDER

Sonic Boom and her young are the only Skylanders to fight as a family. The family that defends the galaxy together, stays together!

STARTING STATS

MAX HEALTH	280
SPEED	50
ARMOR	18
CRITICAL HIT	30
ELEMENTAL POWER	25

PERSONALITY FILE

BRAVE
CUNNING
MATERNAL
HEROIC

POWERS & UPGRADES

STARTING POWERS

ACTION BUTTON

Roar–Lets out a deafening SHRIEK!

ATTACK BUTTON

Egg Toss–Tosses an egg that hatches into an angry baby

POWER UPGRADES

500 GOLD COINS

Loudmouth–Increased damage with her Roar attack

700 GOLD COINS

Let There be Flight!–Increased armor and speed while in flight

900 GOLD COINS

Ride of the Valkyries–Babies take flight and travel at mega speeds

1200 GOLD COINS

Three's a Crowd–Three babies are active at once for toddler terror

"CHOOSE YOUR PATH" UPGRADES

PATH 1: MEDEA GRIFFIN

If you choose this path, Sonic Boom will have even more Griffin baby options.

1700 GOLD COINS

Sunny Side Up–Throws three eggs at once to leave foes with egg on their faces

2200 GOLD COINS

Sibling Rivalry–Four Griffin ankle-biters are active at once

3000 GOLD COINS

Terrible Twos–These babies hatch fully grown. It's man-baby time!

PATH 2: SIREN GRIFFIN

If you choose this path, you will increase Sonic Boom's roar attack.

1700 GOLD COINS

Echolocation–Roar attack increases on impact

2200 GOLD COINS

Egg Shocker–Roaring at eggs generates huge shock waves (and funny looks from passersby)

3000 GOLD COINS

More Boom!–Guaranteed to have neighbors banging on the walls

CYNDER

"VOLTS OF LIGHTNING!"

Although she has a dark past, Cynder caught my attention after joining Spyro on a perilous adventure.

STARTING STATS

MAX HEALTH	260
SPEED	43
ARMOR	18
CRITICAL HIT	30
ELEMENTAL POWER	25

PERSONALITY FILE

SHADY PAST
FIGHTS FOR GOOD
HOPE
INNER DARKNESS

POWERS & UPGRADES

ACTION BUTTON

Spectral Lightning–Shock enemies with lightning bolts

ATTACK BUTTON

Shadow Dash–Sprint forward as a shadow, like an angry goth

POWER UPGRADES

500 GOLD COINS

Cynder Flight–It's time to take to the skies!

700 GOLD COINS

Black Lightning–Cause excess damage with Spectral Lightning

900 GOLD COINS

Double Spooky!–Create ghosts to cause ghoulish damage

1200 GOLD COINS

Shadow Reach–It's like Shadow Dash, but longer!

"CHOOSE YOUR PATH" UPGRADES

PATH 1: NETHER WELDER

If you choose this path, you will increase Cynder's Spectral Lightning attack options.

1700 GOLD COINS

Unstable Forces–Strikes a ghost with Spectral Lightning to make it explode and inflict damage

2200 GOLD COINS

Breath Control–Hold the duration of the lightning strike for longer

3000 GOLD COINS

Breath of Power–Take bad breath to the extreme!

PATH 2: SHADOWDANCER

If you choose this path, you will enhance Cynder's Ghost and Shadow Dash options.

1700 GOLD COINS

Death Bound–Strikes enemies with bad ghosts. Wooooo!

2200 GOLD COINS

Comet Dash–Ghosts with greater endurance, for that extra-annoying haunting

3000 GOLD COINS

Shadow Strike–Shadow Dash does increased damage, like an even angrier goth

SUNBURN

"ROAST-N-TOAST!"

This rare hybrid has the power to match any Skylander. He has all his foes reaching for SPF 50 sunblock.

STARTING STATS

MAX HEALTH	280
SPEED	43
ARMOR	24
CRITICAL HIT	30
ELEMENTAL POWER	25

PERSONALITY FILE

UNIQUE BEING
TELEPORTAL POWERS
PRANKSTER
A-LIST CELEBRITY

POWERS & UPGRADES

STARTING POWERS

ACTION BUTTON

Flamethrower Breath–Blast enemies with a scorchy sizzle

ATTACK BUTTON

Immolation Teleport–Teleport while leaving a flame

POWER UPGRADES

500 GOLD COINS

Guided Teleportation– Teleportal control upgrade

700 GOLD COINS

Blazethrower–Fiery Flamethrower Breath does extra damage

900 GOLD COINS

Phoenix Dash–It's an ultra sprint in the Phoenix Dash

1200 GOLD COINS

Immolation Inflammation– Flames released upon teleporting cause extra damage

"CHOOSE YOUR PATH" UPGRADES

PATH 1: BLAZE DRAGON
If you choose this path, you will increase Sunburn's flamethrower attacks.

1700 GOLD COINS

Infinite Flame–For endless use of fire breath. Handy at a barbecue!

2200 GOLD COINS

Intense Heat–Allows the Flamethower Breath to sustain for longer. Even handier!

3000 GOLD COINS

Phoenix Grand Blaze–Become surrounded by flames (and potentially ruined sausages)

PATH 2: FLAME LORD
If you choose this path, you will develop Sunburn's teleportation skills.

1700 GOLD COINS

Immolation Destruction– Larger flames are left behind after teleporting

2200 GOLD COINS

Flame Streaks–Streaks of flames are generated when teleporting, causing extra damage

3000 GOLD COINS

Burning Trail–Streaks of red flames that are too hot to handle

DOUBLE TROUBLE

"BOOM SHOCK-A-LAKA!"

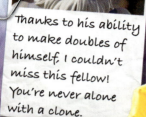

Thanks to his ability to make doubles of himself, I couldn't miss this fellow! You're never alone with a clone.

STARTING STATS		
MAX HEALTH		250
SPEED		35
ARMOR		18
CRITICAL HIT		50
ELEMENTAL POWER		25

PERSONALITY FILE

SPELLCASTER
MAGIC OBSESSION
IMPATIENT
FAR FROM UNIQUE!

POWERS & UPGRADES

STARTING POWERS

ACTION BUTTON

Eldritch Beam—Fires a beam of energy

ATTACK BUTTON

Conjure Exploding Double—A double appears and explodes

POWER UPGRADES

500 GOLD COINS

Arcane Eldritch Beam—Increases damage caused by Eldritch Beam

700 GOLD COINS

Conjure Unstable Double—For clones with anger management problems

900 GOLD COINS

Summon Magic Bomb—Does exactly that . . . summons a bomb!

1200 GOLD COINS

Advanced Construct Techniques—Mo' doubles, mo' problems!

"CHOOSE YOUR PATH" UPGRADES

PATH 1: CHANNELER

If you choose this path, Double Trouble will have even stronger beams and bombs.

1700 GOLD COINS

Extended Eldritch Beam—For that extralong beam

2200 GOLD COINS

Magical Cataclysm—Magic Bombs do more harm

3000 GOLD COINS

Magic Armageddon—Unleash continual Magic Bombs

PATH 2: CONJUROR

Choose this path to provide Double Trouble with even scarier micro doubles.

1700 GOLD COINS

Imbue Construct—Micro doubles increase in size–and antisocial behavior

2200 GOLD COINS

Rocket Powered Doubles—Micro doubles launch toward your foes to inflict extra pain

3000 GOLD COINS

Spirit Construct—Micro doubles continue to form as enemies are defeated

DINO-RANG

"COME 'RANG OR SHINE!"

He destroyed two dark wizards with his twin boomerangs before exploring and finding me.

STARTING STATS

MAX HEALTH	300
SPEED	43
ARMOR	30
CRITICAL HIT	30
ELEMENTAL POWER	25

PERSONALITY FILE

HUNTER
WARRIOR
HOPEFUL
OPTIMISTIC

POWERS & UPGRADES

STARTINGPOWERS

ACTION BUTTON

Stone Boomerangs–Hurls boomerangs at the enemy

ATTACK BUTTON

Boomerang Shield–Destroys foes at close range with this double boomerang attack

POWERUPGRADES

500 GOLD COINS

Basalt Boomerangs–Causes increased boomerang damage

700 GOLD COINS

Boomerang Finesse–Allows control of boomerangs once they've been thrown

900 GOLD COINS

Stonefist Traps–Summons twin stonefists from the earth

1200 GOLD COINS

Dervish Shield–Blocks enemy attacks while doing extra damage

"CHOOSE YOUR PATH"UPGRADES

PATH 1: GRAND BOOMERANG MASTER
Choose this path to strengthen Dino-Rang's boomerang attacks.

1700 GOLD COINS

Volcanic Glass Boomerang–Boomerangs inflict even more mega damage

2200 GOLD COINS

Dancing Boomerangs–These boomerangs ricochet off walls–and the enemy

3000 GOLD COINS

It's All in the Wrist–The Boomerang Shield has increased duration

PATH 2: EARTHEN AVENGER
If you choose this path, you develop Dino-Rang's defensive options.

1700 GOLD COINS

Quad Stonefist Trap–Create four stonefists simultaneously

2200 GOLD COINS

Obsidian Armor–A devilishly handsome new look–with added protection

3000 GOLD COINS

Fist Trap Funeral–Gives enemies a hand–by replacing them with giant fists!

HEX
"FEAR THE DARK!"

With her spooky stare and fondness for skulls, Hex finds it tough to make friends— but she is a most valuable ally.

STARTING STATS

MAX HEALTH	270
SPEED	43
ARMOR	18
CRITICAL HIT	30
ELEMENTAL POWER	25

PERSONALITY FILE

MYSTERIOUS
MENTALLY STRONG
LOOKS GOOD IN BLACK
TRUSTWORTHY

POWERS & UPGRADES

ACTION BUTTON

Conjure Phantom Orb–Track enemies with magic orbs of spectral energy

ATTACK BUTTON

Rain of Skulls–It's raining skulls. Hallelujah!

POWER UPGRADES

500 GOLD COINS

Wall of Bones–Constructs a wall of bones

700 GOLD COINS

Storm of Skulls–Produce up to four skulls with your Rain of Skulls assault

900 GOLD COINS

Bone Fortress–Much larger Wall of Bones that's harder to breach

1200 GOLD COINS

Twice the Orbage–Fire twin orbs simultaneously

"CHOOSE YOUR PATH" UPGRADES

PATH 1: SHADE MASTER
If you choose this path, you will increase Hex's Phantom Orb attack skills.

1700 GOLD COINS

Long Distance Orbs–Lengthen the range of those orbs

2200 GOLD COINS

Caustic Phantom Orbs–Phantom orbs inflict greater damage

3000 GOLD COINS

Unstable Phantom Orbs–For exploding orbs that take out nearby enemies

PATH 2: BONE CRAFTER
If you choose this path, you will increase Hex's Rain of Skulls and Wall of Bones abilities.

1700 GOLD COINS

Compound Fracture–Enemies are damaged upon touching the Wall of Bones

2200 GOLD COINS

Master Caster–Shortens the time it takes to conjure up a Wall of Bones or Rain of Skulls

3000 GOLD COINS

Troll Skulls–Stay a-head (arf!) with this magnified Rain of Skulls

ELEMENT
AIR
SKYLANDER

WHIRLWIND
"TWISTS OF FURY!"

I still remember the first time I saw that amazing rainbow that led me to Whirlwind. She's now a powerful Skylander who leaves evildoers shaking.

STARTING STATS	
MAX HEALTH	270
SPEED	50
ARMOR	18
CRITICAL HIT	50
ELEMENTAL POWER	25

PERSONALITY FILE

LONER
STRONG-WINGED
WILD
FEROCIOUS

POWERS & UPGRADES

STARTING POWERS

ACTION BUTTON

Rainbow of Doom–For a technicolor dream arch

ATTACK BUTTON

Tempest Cloud–Cloudy with a chance of pain!

POWER UPGRADES

500 GOLD COINS

Rainbow Chain–Creates a second rainbow when bounced off a Tempest Cloud

700 GOLD COINS

Triple Tempest–With three Tempest Clouds activated you can create more damage

900 GOLD COINS

Dragon Flight–Gives Whirlwind the ability to fly

1200 GOLD COINS

Duel Rainbows–Deploys a Tempest Cloud and twin rainbows will bounce off it

"CHOOSE YOUR PATH" UPGRADES

PATH 1: ULTIMATE RAINBOWER
If you choose this path, you will increase Whirlwind's Rainbow of Doom abilities.

1700 GOLD COINS

Double Dose of Doom–Fires twin Rainbows of Doom at the same time

2200 GOLD COINS

Atomic Rainbow–Gives more power and increases ability to destroy

3000 GOLD COINS

Rainbow Singularity–This powerful Rainbow of Doom looks lovely–unless you're a bad guy!

PATH 2: TEMPEST DRAGON
Choose this path to add to Whirlwind's Tempest Cloud skills.

1700 GOLD COINS

Triple Rainbow–It's both a weapon and a charming photo opportunity

2200 GOLD COINS

Tempest Tantrum–Prepare for the "painy season" with this extralarge cloud

3000 GOLD COINS

Tempest Matrix–Tempest Clouds become connected by electricity. Shocking!

BOOMER

"BRING THE BOOM!"

Boomer may love blowing up sheep, but he also abandoned the troll army to fight for good—so I had to have him as a Skylander.

STARTING STATS

MAX HEALTH	230
SPEED	35
ARMOR	18
CRITICAL HIT	50
ELEMENTAL POWER	25

PERSONALITY FILE

PYROMANIAC
KIND
THOUGHTFUL
SHEEP-LOVER (SORT OF)

POWERS & UPGRADES

STARTING POWERS

ACTION BUTTON

Dynamite Toss-Toss a stick of special troll dynamite

ATTACK BUTTON

Troll Smash-A ground smash that knocks foes off their feet

POWER UPGRADES

500 GOLD COINS

Dynamite Fuse Fake-Out-Increase dynamite strength. Ka-blam!

700 GOLD COINS

Bash Smash-Increase ground smash to send foes stumbling even farther

900 GOLD COINS

Troll Bomb-Watch out! It's a sizzling Troll Bomb!

1200 GOLD COINS

Triple Bundle Dynamite-Get extra boom for your buck

"CHOOSE YOUR PATH" UPGRADES

PATH 1: DEMOLITION TROLL

Choose this path to increase Boomer's dynamite and Troll Bomb attacks.

1700 GOLD COINS

Bomblastic-Increased bomb damage, reduced health, and safety compliance

2200 GOLD COINS

Troll Bombs Away-Woah! It's six active Troll Bombs at once

3000 GOLD COINS

An Accident Waiting to Happen-Hurl three dynamite sticks at once

PATH 2: CLOBBER TROLL

If you choose this path, you develop Boomer's smash attack skills.

1700 GOLD COINS

Havoc Smash-A smash with even more impact

2200 GOLD COINS

Stupification Smash-A smash that will stun the enemies

3000 GOLD COINS

Megaton Charged Super Smash-Charge it up and unleash the ultra smash!

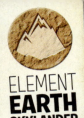

TERRAFIN

"IT'S FEEDING TIME!"

Terrafin is an ex-lifeguard who is trained in the art of boxing. I discovered him at one of his prize fights and knew I could put his talents to better use.

STARTING STATS

MAX HEALTH	310
SPEED	35
ARMOR	18
CRITICAL HIT	30
ELEMENTAL POWER	25

PERSONALITY FILE

PROTECTIVE
DETERMINED
BOXER
BOTH A LOVER AND A FIGHTER

POWERS & UPGRADES

STARTING POWERS

ACTION BUTTON

Punch–Throw that fist and go for the KO

ATTACK BUTTON

Earth Swim–Burrow underground first, ask questions later

POWER UPGRADES

500 GOLD COINS

Brass Knuckles–Punches have, well, extra punch!

700 GOLD COINS

Mega Bellyflop–Unleash some tummy-based terror

900 GOLD COINS

Feeding Frenzy–Mini-sharks launch into action and start burrowing

1200 GOLD COINS

Multi Target Punches–These punches take out numerous enemies at once

"CHOOSE YOUR PATH" UPGRADES

PATH 1: SANDHOG

If you choose this path, you will increase Terrafin's Earth Swim skills.

1700 GOLD COINS

Master Earth Swimmer–For superfast burrowing

2200 GOLD COINS

Homing Frenzy–The mini-sharks hone in on enemies before dishing out fishy fury

3000 GOLD COINS

Razorfin–While underground, the dorsal fin gets a slice of the action. Shaaark!!

PATH 2: BRAWLER

Choose this path to give Terrafin an even more powerful Punch attack.

1700 GOLD COINS

Pugilist–It's time to perform a mega body slam

2200 GOLD COINS

Spiked Knuckles–It's like a punch . . . but with spikes! Ouch!

3000 GOLD COINS

Frenzy Shield–Any enemy who hurts you will automatically have mini-sharks unleashed on them

SLAM BAM

"ARMED AND DANGEROUS!"

Slam Bam was drifting through the skies before landing on my island. I saw his incredible abilities and made him an offer he couldn't refuse.

STARTING STATS	
MAX HEALTH	310
SPEED	35
ARMOR	30
CRITICAL HIT	10
ELEMENTAL POWER	25

PERSONALITY FILE

NATURAL LONER
ARTISTIC
POWERFUL
SNOW CONE GENIUS

POWERS & UPGRADES

STARTING POWERS

ACTION BUTTON

Yeti Fists–Unleashes punches with all four freezy fists at once

ATTACK BUTTON

Ice Prison–Trap the enemy in a chilly ice prison. Brrr!

POWER UPGRADES

500 GOLD COINS

Three's a Charm–Activate three ice prisons at the same time

700 GOLD COINS

Arctic Explosion–It's "ice, ice, baby" in these exploding ice prisons!

900 GOLD COINS

Yeti Ice Shoe Slide–It's a mega slide across the ground! Wheee!

1200 GOLD COINS

Ice Knuckles–Cause extra damage with these ice knuckles

"CHOOSE YOUR PATH" UPGRADES

PATH 1: BLIZZARD BRAWLER
Choose this path to increase Slam Bam's Yeti Fists attack.

1700 GOLD COINS

Brawler Combos–Launch an attack with an ice hammer. Ouch!

2200 GOLD COINS

Ice Mace–These ultimate punches cause even more damage

3000 GOLD COINS

Blizzard Battle Armor–Gain extra protection (and not by just wearing a nice scarf)

PATH 2: GLACIER HIT
If you choose this path, Slam Bam will develop his Ice Prison abilities.

1700 GOLD COINS

Deep Chill Ice Coffin–These ice prisons cause harm to those trapped inside

2200 GOLD COINS

Glacier Tactics–Ice prisons travel even farther and at top speeds

3000 GOLD COINS

Work of Ice Art–Ice prisons endure for longer, making enemies wish they'd packed warmer clothes

ELEMENT
MAGIC
SKYLANDER

WRECKING BALL

"WRECK-N-ROLL!"

This Skylander literally rolled into my life and instantly reminded me of my favorite childhood pet. I named him myself and made him a Skylander. Awww!

PERSONALITY FILE

GREEDY
OPPORTUNIST
DESTRUCTIVE
RECKLESS

POWERS & UPGRADES

STARTING POWERS

ACTION BUTTON

Tongue Whap–Give enemies a licking

ATTACK BUTTON

Forcefield Ball–Ever wanted to be a marauding blue meatball? Now's your chance

POWER UPGRADES

500 GOLD COINS

Magic Ball Control–Control the Forcefield Ball to do extra harm

700 GOLD COINS

Power Belch–It's disgusting but effective!

900 GOLD COINS

Tongue Evolution–Increased tongue length for increased lickage

1200 GOLD COINS

Digestive Detonation–Part deadly weapon, part disgusting habit

"CHOOSE YOUR PATH" UPGRADES

PATH 1: TOTAL TONGUE
Choose this path to add to Wrecking Ball's tongue attack options.

1700 GOLD COINS

Lightning Tongue–It's a tongue attack at lightning speed. And it's not pretty

2200 GOLD COINS

Tongue Grabber–Tongue can pick up food and power-ups, plus do extra damage

3000 GOLD COINS

Tongue Supermax–This is one mega long tongue!

PATH 2: ULTIMATE SPINNER
If you choose this path, you will create better forcefield attacks.

1700 GOLD COINS

Forcefield Blast–Don't try this at home! Or any of the others, come to think of it

2200 GOLD COINS

Swath of Terror–Increase Forcefield Ball damage

3000 GOLD COINS

It's Gotta Go Somewhere–It's a mega burp attack, unleashed from within the Forcefield Ball

DRILL SERGEANT

"LICENSED TO DRILL!"

I performed some magic to bring this ancient Arkeyan machine back to life after he was found by Terrafin. His new task is to defend the world as a Skylander.

STARTING STATS	
MAX HEALTH	290
SPEED	43
ARMOR	12
CRITICAL HIT	30
ELEMENTAL POWER	25

PERSONALITY FILE

STRONG
GRATEFUL
OBEDIENT
DETERMINED

POWERS & UPGRADES

ACTION BUTTON

Drill Rocket–Fire exploding homing rockets at the enemy

ATTACK BUTTON

Bulldoze Charge–Unleash a relentless charge

POWER UPGRADES

500 GOLD COINS

A Speedy Recovery–Drill Rockets are on super reload

700 GOLD COINS

Dozer Endurance–Increase time in the Bulldoze Charge mode

900 GOLD COINS

Power Charge–Increase Bulldoze Charge power

1200 GOLD COINS

Auto-Blaster–It's time to activate an Arkeyan secret weapon

"CHOOSE YOUR PATH" UPGRADES

PATH 1: BATTLEDOZER
If you choose this path, you will increase Drill Sergeant's Drill Rocket attack options.

1700 GOLD COINS

A View to a Drill–Increased Drill Rocket attack (also useful for DIY)

2200 GOLD COINS

DX3000-Drill Detonator–Drills release an area of explosive pulse

3000 GOLD COINS

MIRV Drill Rockets–Drill Rockets morph into a series of smaller rockets

PATH 2: MEGADOZER
If you choose this path, you will add to Drill Sergeant's charge and Auto-Blaster attacks.

1700 GOLD COINS

Speed Dozer Boost–A superspeed bulldoze charge

2200 GOLD COINS

Hail Storm–Ssh! The Arkeyan secret weapon just cranked up a notch!

3000 GOLD COINS

Mega Dozer–Look out! It's the ultimate bulldozer

DROBOT

"BLINK AND DESTROY!"

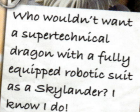

Who wouldn't want a supertechnical dragon with a fully equipped robotic suit as a Skylander? I know I do!

STARTING STATS

MAX HEALTH	290
SPEED	43
ARMOR	24
CRITICAL HIT	20
ELEMENTAL POWER	25

PERSONALITY FILE

SUPERSMART
TECHNICAL
NATURALLY WEAK FLYER
BELIEF

POWERS & UPGRADES

STARTING POWERS

ACTION BUTTON

Mega Blasters–Blast laser beams from the eyes

ATTACK BUTTON

Tactical Bladegears–Fire spinning bladegears to slice and dice

POWER UPGRADES

500 GOLD COINS

Thruster Flight–Take flight with robotic suit thrusters

700 GOLD COINS

Galvanized Bladegears– Here come some mega bladegears!

900 GOLD COINS

Axon Focus Crystals–Cause extra damage with eye-blasting beams

1200 GOLD COINS

Hover Mode–Take flight and hover in midair

"CHOOSE YOUR PATH" UPGRADES

PATH 1: MASTER BLASTER
If you choose this path, you will add extra fury to Drobot's eye blaster attack.

1700 GOLD COINS

Dendrite Focus Crystals–Give the enemy the evil eye

2200 GOLD COINS

Antimatter Charges–Laser beams explode upon impact. There's no escaping them!

3000 GOLD COINS

Quadratic Blasters–What?! Fire laser beams from the wings as well? If you insist!

PATH 2: CLOCKWORK DRAGON
Choose this path to boost Drobot's bladegear options.

1700 GOLD COINS

Depleted Uranium Bladegears–Inflict ultra damage with these upgraded bladegears

2200 GOLD COINS

Explosive Bladegears– Bladegears explode on impact causing increased damage

3000 GOLD COINS

Tri-Spread Bladegears–Unleash three bladegears at the same time

WARNADO

"FOR THE WIND!"

When he first hatched, Warnado was permanently frightened. Now he's the most powerful turtle I've ever known (and, in case you're wondering, I've known a few!).

STARTING STATS

MAX HEALTH	310
SPEED	35
ARMOR	30
CRITICAL HIT	10
ELEMENTAL POWER	25

PERSONALITY FILE

POWERFUL
IMPATIENT
FAST-THINKING
STRONG

POWERS & UPGRADES

STARTING POWERS

ACTION BUTTON

Spin Attack–By spinning inside your shell you can destroy enemies.

ATTACK BUTTON

Summon Tornado–Lift enemies into the air with a superspin

POWER UPGRADES

500 GOLD COINS

500

Sharp Shell–Maximize damage (and dizziness!) with a Spin Attack

700 GOLD COINS

700

Whirlwind Flight–Increase air-bound speed and armor

900 GOLD COINS

900

Extend Tornado–Create even more damage with a mega tornado

1200 GOLD COINS

1200

High Winds–You can eliminate multiple enemies with these tornadoes

"CHOOSE YOUR PATH" UPGRADES

PATH 1: EYE OF THE STORM
Upgrade to this path and hone Warnado's Spin Attack and flying skills.

1700 GOLD COINS

1700

Low Friction Shell–Shoots much farther, not to mention quicker

2200 GOLD COINS

2200

Flying Mini-Turtles–Attack enemies with flying Mini-Warnados

3000 GOLD COINS

3000

Turtle Slam–Crush the enemy by landing on them with a satisfying thud

PATH 2: WIND MASTER
Take the enemy by storm with this upgrade path that helps develop Warnado's tornado attacks.

1700 GOLD COINS

1700

Guided Twister–Get full control of your tornado

2200 GOLD COINS

2200

Summon Cyclone–Create more destruction with an oversized tornado

3000 GOLD COINS

3000

Wind Elemental–Tornadoes work independently of you to take out the enemy

I convinced this little Skylander to help protect our world after seeing his fruit-exploding gift with my very own eyes.

CAMO

"FRUIT PUNCH!"

STARTING STATS

MAX HEALTH	300
SPEED	50
ARMOR	34
CRITICAL HIT	30
ELEMENTAL POWER	25

PERSONALITY FILE

EXPLOSIVE
ENERGETIC
HOTHEADED
STRONG LEADER

POWERS & UPGRADES

STARTING POWERS

ACTION BUTTON

Sun Burst-Take out enemies with a concentrated firebolt

ATTACK BUTTON

Firecracker Vines-Quickly grow a vine of volatile fruit

POWER UPGRADES

500 GOLD COINS

Searing Sun Blast-Maximize damage with an increased Sun Burst

700 GOLD COINS

Melon Fountain-Spray melons for juicy, delicious destuction. Mmm!

900 GOLD COINS

Firecracker Food-How d'ya like them apples? Not much as it happens

1200 GOLD COINS

Vigorous Vines-These vines shoot through the air even quicker

"CHOOSE YOUR PATH" UPGRADES

PATH 1: VINE VIRTUOSO
If you choose this path, you will increase Camo's abilities with Firecracker Vines.

1700 GOLD COINS

Martial Bounty-Firecracker Vines produce awesome combusting peppers

2200 GOLD COINS

Peppers of Potency-Do massive damage with these Firecracker Vines

3000 GOLD COINS

Proliferation-Make twin Firecracker Vines

PATH 2: MELON MASTER
If you choose this path, you will increase Camo's enviable Melon Fountain skill set.

1700 GOLD COINS

Ring of Might-A melon-producing fountain-which isn't something you see every day

2200 GOLD COINS

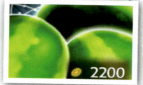

Melon GMO-Proving that fruit isn't always good for you

3000 GOLD COINS

Melon Fortress-Seek cover in the fountain before unleashing fruity mayhem

ZOOK

"LOCKED-AND-LOADED!"

This Skylander earned my respect after I saw his love for his fellow Bambazookers—and impressive carving skills!

STARTING STATS

MAX HEALTH	260
SPEED	43
ARMOR	30
CRITICAL HIT	20
ELEMENTAL POWER	25

PERSONALITY FILE

PROTECTIVE
SECRETIVE
PEACE-LOVING
RESOURCEFUL

POWERS & UPGRADES

STARTING POWERS

ACTION BUTTON

Bazooka Attack-Shoot shells that splinter into little pieces

ATTACK BUTTON

Foliage Barrier-Grow a wall of bamboo to protect yourself (might not work against pandas)

POWER UPGRADES

500 GOLD COINS

Hardwood Shells-Increase damage with disintegrating Bazooka Attack

700 GOLD COINS

Fungal Bloom-Thicker Foliage Barrier increases protection

900 GOLD COINS

Mortar Attack-Rain shells down on your enemy

1200 GOLD COINS

Full Splinter Jacket-Produce more shrapnel with these supershells

"CHOOSE YOUR PATH" UPGRADES

PATH 1: ARTILLERYMAN

If you choose this path, you will increase Zook's Bazooka Attack talents.

1700 GOLD COINS

High Velocity Shrapnel-Extend range of shrapnel

2200 GOLD COINS

Old Growth Bazooka-Increase weapon damage

3000 GOLD COINS

Exploding Shrapnel-Deploys shrapnel on contact destroying more enemies

PATH 2: FLORAL DEFENDER

Opt for this path if you wish to increase Zook's Cactus Barrier abilities.

1700 GOLD COINS

Cactus Barrier - All who touch it are dealt a thorny surprise

2200 GOLD COINS

Mortar of Life - Mortar detonates and produces a cactus

3000 GOLD COINS

Fightin' Foliage - When plants attack!

WHAM-SHELL

"BRACE FOR THE MACE!"

ELEMENT
WATER
SKYLANDER

The tale of Wham-Shell's courageous victory over the trolls did not take long to reach me. I had no choice but to reach out an arm to this heroic, crustacean prince.

STARTING STATS	
MAX HEALTH	300
SPEED	50
ARMOR	18
CRITICAL HIT	30
ELEMENTAL POWER	25

PERSONALITY FILE

REGAL
DETERMINED
COURAGEOUS
HEROIC

POWERS & UPGRADES

ACTION BUTTON

Malacostracan Mace–He might not be able to say it, but he can sure use it!

ATTACK BUTTON

Starfish Bullets–The magic mace fires starfish bullets

POWER UPGRADES

500 GOLD COINS

Starfishicus Giganticus–Extracharged Starfish Bullets Attack

700 GOLD COINS

King's Mace–Enlarged mace inflicts extra damage

900 GOLD COINS

Starfishicus Superioralis–It's an increased power starfish attack

1200 GOLD COINS

Poseidon Strike–The mace creates an electric field that harms the enemy

"CHOOSE YOUR PATH" UPGRADES

PATH 1: CAPTAIN CRUSTACEAN
This path allows Wham-Shell to develop his mace skills.

1700 GOLD COINS

Crustacean Combos–It's time to unleash the Mace Master attack

2200 GOLD COINS

Mega Trident–Ultra damage with this mace attack upgrade

3000 GOLD COINS

Mace of the Deep–Unleash a powerful Poseidon strike

PATH 2: COMMANDER CRAB
If you choose this path, you increase Wham-Shell's starfish bullet options.

1700 GOLD COINS

Triplicate Starfish–Fire three starfish bullets simultaneously

2200 GOLD COINS

Semi-Eternal Pursuit–These starfish seek out the enemies

3000 GOLD COINS

Nightmare Huggers–Starfish cling to the enemy in a way that's both hurtful and embarrassing

LIGHTNING ROD

"ONE STRIKE AND YOU'RE OUT!"

The moment Spyro brought Rod to see me, I knew that this chiseled hero would be an awesome asset to our cause. And I'm a sucker for a well-groomed beard!

STARTING STATS	
MAX HEALTH	290
SPEED	43
ARMOR	18
CRITICAL HIT	30
ELEMENTAL POWER	25

PERSONALITY FILE

CHARMING
BRAVE
HEROIC
CHARISMATIC

POWERS & UPGRADES

POWER UPGRADES

500 GOLD COINS

Lightning Lancer–A bolt from the blue with magnified damage

700 GOLD COINS

Thunderation–Keep your pets indoors from this sustained attack!

900 GOLD COINS

Zapper Field–Summon an electric storm to wipe out the enemy

1200 GOLD COINS

Lightning Harpoon–This will definitely hurt in the morning

"CHOOSE YOUR PATH" UPGRADES

PATH 1: LIGHTNING LORD

If you choose this path, you will add to Lightning Rod's Grand Lightning Summoning attacks.

1700 GOLD COINS

Faster Caster–Conjure up lightning a lot faster

2200 GOLD COINS

Electricity City–Super lightning blitz increases power and damage

3000 GOLD COINS

Lightning Avatar–Call upon the greatest lightning attack available

PATH 2: TYPHOON TITAN

If you choose this, path Lightning Rod will be bestowed with extra cloud defense skills.

1700 GOLD COINS

Cloud Zapper Satellite–A cloud that both shields you and fires on enemies

2200 GOLD COINS

Zapper Sats–Zapper cloud shield inflicts more devastation

3000 GOLD COINS

Zapper Satellite Defense– Protect yourself with three zapper clouds

GHOST ROASTER
"NO CHAIN, NO GAIN!"

This chef-turned-ghoul has not only proven himself worthy as a Skylander, but also whips up a mean fish curry (which only sometimes contains bones).

STARTING STATS	
MAX HEALTH	280
SPEED	43
ARMOR	24
CRITICAL HIT	20
ELEMENTAL POWER	25

PERSONALITY FILE

DETERMINED
UNDYING APPETITE
RELENTLESS
GOOD IN THE KITCHEN

POWERS & UPGRADES

STARTING POWERS

ACTION BUTTON

Chain Whip–Fling the spiked ball to destroy enemies

ATTACK BUTTON

Skull Charge–Chomp through the enemy as a giant skull

POWER UPGRADES

500 GOLD COINS

Pain Chain–Spiked ball does mega damage

700

Metalhead–Increase the length of your skull attacks

900 GOLD COINS

Ectoplasm Mode–This health-sucking mode gives you protection from enemies

1200 GOLD COINS

Haunt–Turn the enemies to your side with the Chain Whip

"CHOOSE YOUR PATH" UPGRADES

PATH 1: FEAR EATER
If you choose this path, you will increase Ghost Roaster's Ectoplasm Mode skill set. And who wouldn't want to do that?

1700 GOLD COINS

Phase Shift Burst–Treat your enemies to an extra dose of slime

2200 GOLD COINS

Ecto-Friendly–Limit the loss of health and increase speed while in Ectoplasm Mode

3000 GOLD COINS

Nightmare Touch–Create explosions upon contact with enemies while in Ectoplasm Mode

PATH 2: SKULL MASTER
If you choose this path, you will increase Ghost Roaster's Skull Charge abilities.

1700 GOLD COINS

Fright Bite–Maximize damage when in Skull Charge mode

2200 GOLD COINS

Unfinished Business–Enemies destroyed in Skull Charge will become ghosts

3000 GOLD COINS

Life Transfer–Eat a ghost and feel the benefit. It's the new dieting craze!

FLYNN

"CALI? AAH CALI!"

This Mabu is unlike any other, both in looks and personality. He's like a glorified taxi driver, giving fellow Mabu rides between floating islands. Although he has an inflated opinion of himself, he does have a good heart and is extremely optimistic. He lends himself and his balloon to good causes and is ready and willing to help any Skylander who needs transportation. Provided he can tear himself away from his first love, Cali, that is.

 Flynn is full of bravado but with a heart of gold!

PERSONALITY FILE

FRIENDLY
CONFIDENT
OUTGOING

HUGO

"WE HAVE MUCH TO DO!"

My faithful assistant knows much of our world's history. At least, that's what he tells me.

Hugo had loyally served me for many years and survived the destruction of the Core of Light by hiding underground. Hugo has a vast knowledge of the history of Skylands and is a great source of information. He is not a fighter and a little cowardly, but this is because he is rather small, fairly weak, and pretty uncoordinated. Oh well! You can't have everything.

PERSONALITY FILE

BUMBLING
LOYAL
KNOWLEDGEABLE

KAOS

This evil Portal Master prefers to be seen as a large, projected head—for reasons that are obvious to all who have met him.

My archnemesis, Kaos, may be annoying and have appalling dress sense, but he also possesses immense power. It was he who harnessed the power of the Darkness and destroyed the Core of Light, causing the Skylanders to be banished and frozen. Not bad for a day's work, even I have to admit. Do not underestimate him, no matter how tempting it is.

PERSONALITY FILE
BIG EGO
ANNOYING
POWER-SEEKING

GLUMSHANKS

The doomed sidekick to the most bigheaded Portal Master there is!

Glumshanks is Kaos' goblin sidekick. He has always been loyal and faithful to his evil master, even though he is often in despair over his hair-brained plans and terrible jokes.

PERSONALITY FILE
FAITHFUL
LOYAL
DESPAIRING

KNOW YOUR ENEMY

Red alert! And green alert! And all other possible colors of alert, for that matter. This gaggle of nasties stands between you and saving the universe—which is naughty of them, to say the least. Study them well if you wish to succeed on your quest.

HP = HEALTH POINTS
XP EARNED = EXPERIENCE POINTS

CHOMPY

First appears in Shattered Island

Chompies may be small, but they're far from cute. Their teeth are so sharp they could be can openers (or entire building openers).

DAMAGE: 11
HP: 1
XP EARNED: 1

CHOMPY POD
First appears in Perilous Pastures

DAMAGE: 1
HP: 61
XP EARNED: 20

DROW WITCH
First appears in Sky Schooner Docks

DAMAGE: 19
HP: 40
XP EARNED: 32

DROW ZEPPELIN
First appears in Sky Schooner Docks

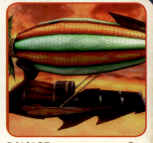

DAMAGE: 9
HP: 10
XP EARNED: 0

AIR SPELL PUNK
First appears in Sky Schooner Docks

DAMAGE: 59
HP: 90
XP EARNED: 105

DROW SPEARMEN
First appears in Perilous Pastures

DAMAGE: 31
HP: 43
XP EARNED: 38

WINDBAG DJINNI
First appears in Stormy Stronghold

DAMAGE: 30
HP: 114
XP EARNED: 70

TECH SPELL PUNK
First appears in Oilspill Island

Some magicians like to make rabbits appear or saw pretty ladies in half. This fellow prefers to summon laser beams from the sky and blast you with them. I prefer the first kind.

DAMAGE: 77
HP: 90
XP EARNED: 102

TROLL GREASEMONKEY
First appears in Oilspill Island

DAMAGE: 12
HP: 31
XP EARNED: 20

BLASTER TROLL
First appears in Oilspill Island

DAMAGE: 34
HP: 40
XP EARNED: 17

TROLL GRENADIER
First appears in Oilspill Island

DAMAGE: 24
HP: 18
XP EARNED: 17

MARK 31 TROLL TANK
First appears in Oilspill Island

DAMAGE: 53
HP: 100
XP EARNED: 0

GOLIATH DROW
First appears in Sky Schooner Docks

DAMAGE: 57
HP: 111
XP EARNED: 128

NAUTELOID
First appears in Dark Water Cove

DAMAGE: 18
HP: 1
XP EARNED: 4

SQUIDFACE BRUTE

First appears in Dark Water Cove

DAMAGE: 91
HP: 136
XP EARNED: 84

WATER SPELL PUNK

First appears in Dark Water Cove

DAMAGE: 73
HP: 99
XP EARNED: 125

SQUIDDLER

First appears in Dark Water

Be sure to turn this fishy oaf into deep-fried squid before he fires an exploding blowfish at you. It's as bad as it sounds.

DAMAGE: 22
HP: 17
XP EARNED: 21

DARK WATER DRAGON

First appears in Leviathan lagoon

DAMAGE: 18
HP: 372
XP EARNED: 180

HOB 'N' YARO

First appears in Leviathan Lagoon

DAMAGE: 73
HP: 49
XP EARNED: 132

BLASTANER

First appears in Dark Water Cove

DAMAGE: 24
HP: 56
XP EARNED: 20

DARK ICE YETI

First appears in Leviathan Lagoon

DAMAGE: 76
HP: 447
XP EARNED: 230

DARK AMPHIBIOUS GILLMAN

First appears in Leviathan Lagoon

DAMAGE: **27**
HP: **298**
XP EARNED: **200**

TIMIDCLOPS

First appears in Crystal Eye Castle

DAMAGE: **36**
HP: **2**
XP EARNED: **32**

CYCLOPS CHOPPER

First appears in Crystal Eye Castle

DAMAGE: **48**
HP: **14**
XP EARNED: **38**

CYCLOPS CHUCKER

First appears in Crystal Eye Castle

DAMAGE: **36**
HP: **54**
XP EARNED: **32**

CYCLOPS MAMMOTH

First appears in Crystal Eye Castle

DAMAGE: **109**
HP: **149**
XP EARNED: **127**

STONE GOLEM

First appears in Stonetown

DAMAGE: **35**
HP: **1000**
XP EARNED: **1600**

EARTH SPELL PUNK

First appears in Stonetown

As if being a Spell Punk isn't bad enough, this one spends his time aiding his fellow fiends by arming them with magical defenses. A real mystic meanie.

DAMAGE: **45**
HP: **81**
XP EARNED: **210**

ROCK WALKER
First appears in Stonetown

DAMAGE:................**60**
HP:........................**74**
XP EARNED:..........**42**

CORN HORNET
First appears in Treetop Terrace

DAMAGE:........................**16**
HP:..................................**23**
XP EARNED:...................**29**

BLADE WITCH
First appears in Treetop Terrace

If there's one thing that's even more bothersome than a wicked witch, it's a wicked witch with a boomerang. Just remember: What goes around, comes around!

DAMAGE:............**33**
HP:........................**35**
XP EARNED:........**29**

DARK NINJA MINION
First appears in Falling Forest

DAMAGE:........................**69**
HP:................................**177**
XP EARNED:.................**370**

DARK MISSILE MINION
First appears in Falling Forest

DAMAGE:........................**63**
HP:................................**294**
XP EARNED:.................**350**

BLITZER BULLY
First appears in Treetop Terrace

DAMAGE:......................**109**
HP:................................**149**
XP EARNED:.................**117**

DARK LIFE MINION
First appears in Falling Forest

DAMAGE:........................**94**
HP:................................**515**
XP EARNED:.................**390**

ROCKET IMP
First appears in Troll Warehouse

DAMAGE: 24
HP: 63
XP EARNED: 53

LAVA KING
First appears in Molekin Mine

DAMAGE: 109
HP: 105
XP EARNED: 46

FAT BELLY SPIDER
First appears in Crawling Catacombs

DAMAGE: 26
HP: 67
XP EARNED: 55

GUN SNOUT
First appears in Troll Warehouse

DAMAGE: 27
HP: 187
XP EARNED: 216

FLAME IMP
First appears in Molekin Mine

Tempting as it may be to have one installed in your home for those chilly winter months, the Flame Imp is not to be trusted. Snuff out his fiery flames at the earliest opportunity.

DAMAGE: 19
HP: 1
XP EARNED: 4

SPIDER SPITTER
First appears in Crawling Catacombs

DAMAGE: 0
HP: 40
XP EARNED: 0

MOON WIDOW
First appears in Crawling Catacombs

DAMAGE: 0
HP: 46
XP EARNED: 66

GARGANTULA

First appears in Crawling Catacombs

DAMAGE: 161
HP: 186
XP EARNED: 220

SPIDER SWARMER

First appears in Crawling Catacombs

DAMAGE: 32
HP: 1
XP EARNED: 4

ROTTING ROBBIE

First appears in Cadaverous Crypt

DAMAGE: 99
HP: 99
XP EARNED: 62

BONE 'N' ARROW

First appears in Cadaverous Crypt

DAMAGE: 30
HP: 49
XP EARNED: 52

UNDEAD SPELL PUNK

First appears in Cadaverous Crypt

This nasty piece of work can summon up pesky Rhu-Babies, who then grow into full-blown Rhu-Barbs. If you ask me, the whole lot of them should be turned into rhubarb crumble.

DAMAGE: **143**
HP: **144**
XP EARNED: **311**

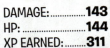

RHU-BARB

First appears in Cadaverous Crypt

DAMAGE: 150
HP: 200
XP EARNED: 62

DARK KNIGHT MINION

First appears in Creepy Citadel

DAMAGE: 80
HP: 470
XP EARNED: 870

DARK IMP MINION

First appears in Creepy Citadel

DAMAGE: 97
HP: 361
XP EARNED: 850

DARK WITCH

First appears in Creepy Citadel

DAMAGE: 66
HP: 397
XP EARNED: 900

SHADOW KNIGHT

First appears in Creepy Citadel

Don't expect this knight to do anything good such as rescue a maiden from a dragon's clutches. The only dragon this swordsman wants to slay is Spyro.

DAMAGE: 89
HP: 199
XP EARNED: 236

DARK PYRO ARCHER

First appears in Lava Lakes Railway

DAMAGE: 49
HP: 192
XP EARNED: 1100

ROCKER WALKER

First appears in Molekin Mine

DAMAGE: 140
HP: 173
XP EARNED: 152

DARK EVIL ERUPTOR

First appears in Lava Lakes Railway

DAMAGE: 98
HP: 480
XP EARNED: 1150

DARK PHOENIX DRAGON

First appears in Lava Lakes Railway

DAMAGE: 54
HP: 384
XP EARNED: 1130

GNASHER
First appears in Quicksilver Vault

Those gnasty gnashers were made for more than just chewing through toffee. Turn him from green and blue to black and blue if you wish to make it past him to (relative) safety.

DAMAGE:............... 19
HP:........................ 1
XP EARNED:.......... 4

MAGIC SPELL PUNK
First appears in Quicksilver Vault

DAMAGE:....................171
HP:...........................81
XP EARNED:.................586

ARKEYAN ULTRON
First appears in Quicksilver Vault

DAMAGE:....................106
HP:...........................279
XP EARNED:.................244

ARKEYAN BLASTER
First appears in Quicksilver Vault

DAMAGE:......................36
HP:...........................61
XP EARNED:..................61

ARKEYAN DEFENDER
First appears in Quicksilver Vault

DAMAGE:......................71
HP:...........................67
XP EARNED:..................73

DEFENSE DRONE
First appears in Arkeyan Armory

DAMAGE:......................21
HP:............................2
XP EARNED:...................4

ARKEYAN WAR MACHINE
First appears in Arkeyan Armory

DAMAGE:....................106
HP:...........................279
XP EARNED:.................244

Exploring SKYLANDS

CHAPTER 1
SHATTERED ISLAND

It's time to enter Skylands for the first time. The first place your chosen Skylander will appear is on Shattered Island. Here you will meet Hugo and Flynn. I have instructed Hugo to be your guide and Flynn will take you on your journey from one island to the next . . . if you don't crash on the way, that is. Good luck with that!

OBJECTIVE
RESCUE THE VILLAGERS

AREAS
FRACTURED VISTA
OLD TOWN
MARKET CURVE
TURTLE GULLY
TURTLE HIDEOUT
CHOMPIE PIT
WHIRLPOOL FALLS
FLOATING MILLS
ANCIENT LANDMARK

ITEMS TO FIND
1 SOUL GEM
1 LEGENDARY TREASURE
3 HATS
3 TREASURE CHESTS
1 STORY SCROLL

Valuable items are hidden in obstacles like barrels and boxes. Blast them all to see what you can find.

HINTS AND TIPS

HINT: Find the cannon to blast through the wall.

📜 FRACTURED VISTA

Calamity! The main road on the island has been destroyed and the first of the town folk to need rescuing are trapped behind a wall of rubble.

OLD TOWN 👉

Once you've demolished the first obstacle, you can enter the Old Town. Here you will receive some advice from a villager called Rizzo.

HINT: Grab the key to unlock the gate and free more villagers. They're always very grateful, so get used to the praise!

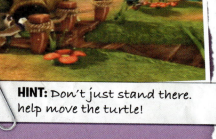

HINT: Don't just stand there, help move the turtle!

📜 MARKET CURVE

Enter Market Curve and find the key to open the gate.

HINT: The key is close to the cannon.

After meeting with Nort (and having a pleasant chat), you'll realize that the bridge over Turtle Gully has been blocked. Oh no! People are trapped on the far side and need rescuing.

MORE **CHAPTER 1 HINTS AND TIPS** ON THE NEXT PAGE!

CHAPTER 1 SHATTERED ISLAND

TURTLE GULLY

Flynn arrives to greet you (if he can land the balloon safely, that is!)

HINT: Reach Flynn by using the bounce pads.

TURTLE HIDEOUT

Wait! Before you use the bounce pads there's somewhere you haven't discovered yet!

HINT: Discover Turtle Hideout by moving the turtle to the left of the bounce pad until it falls into the hole.

Once you've done that, run over the turtle and down the slope.

HINT: You'll need a Magic Skylander to open this one, so if you're playing with Gill Grunt, then snatch him off that Portal of Power. He's a Water Skylander and no use here! Spyro would do the trick.

Use your attack button to smash through debris and obstacles. Ka-pow!

CHOMPIE PIT

Once you've visited Turtle Hideout then leap up those bounce pads to reach Flynn. But watch out! You'll soon be attacked by a twister and plunged into the Chompie Pit while lucky Flynn escapes in the balloon.

HINT: If you can blast those sharp-gnashered Chompies then you'll find a Treasure Chest in there. Once you've destroyed the last of the Chompies, you'll also automatically unlock the gate.

WHIRLPOOL FALLS

With the Chompies gone for now, you can take a leisurely stroll through the gate where you'll discover another Elemental Gate.

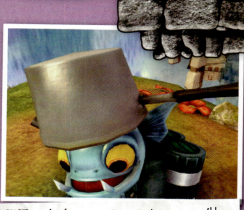

HINT: This is a Water Gate so you'll need a Water Skylander like Gill Grunt or Zap to help you here. Look out for the whirlpool!

FLOATING MILLS

Through the Tech gate and over the bridge is a present that contains a hat. Watch out as you move across the bridge, though. There are spinning blades that would love to inflict some pain on your Health stat.

Once you successfully get back across the bridge and through the gate in one piece, head up the slope.

HINT: Watch out for the Chompies!

ANCIENT LANDMARK

Here you will discover another gate. You are about to get a royal seal of approval, because beyond this gate is the trapped royal family.

HINT: Raid the Treasure Chest and grab the key to unlock the gate.

You have now rescued all the villagers. Yahoo! Now you must escape the scary tornado in Flynn's balloon . . . although Flynn's flying is probably as scary as any twister!

CHAPTER 2
PERILOUS PASTURES

Here we return to the Ruins. This is the place where the Core of Light was destroyed by Kaos. If you're lucky, Flynn will safely land the balloon and allow you to explore. By the way, he'll also start to tell you about Cali. The difficulty is getting him to stop!

OBJECTIVE

FIND CALI

AREAS

SUNFLOWER RIDGE–TECH
BLEATING HIGHLANDS–TECH
FAIRY RING–MAGIC
ANCIENT STONES–WATER
LANDING DECK–LIFE

ITEMS TO FIND

1 SOUL GEM
1 LEGENDARY TREASURE
2 HATS
3 TREASURE CHESTS
1 STORY SCROLL

HINTS AND TIPS

**SUNFLOWER RIDGE**

As soon as you enter Sunflower Ridge you will discover a gate blocking your route. Find the key to continue.

HINT: Make sure you explore through the Tech Gate to the right first!

BLEATING HIGHLANDS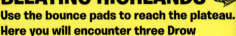

Use the bounce pads to reach the plateau. Here you will encounter three Drow Spearmen and some Chompies.

HINT: A great way to halt the Chompies is to destroy the Chompy Pods. That will stop them from spawning.

FAIRY RING

Defeat the Chompies and collect the Story Scroll. In the turtle-pushing challenge, push the turtles, collect the items, and defeat the Drow Spearmen.

HINT: Go over the turtle bridge you have created to collect a key.

ANCIENT STONES

This area can only be reached through the Water gate. Hop into the whirlpool and travel to this secret area.

HINT: You must find the right order to move the blocks. If you do, you will find a route to the teleport pad.

LANDING DECK

Cali has been captured by Drow Spearmen and needs your help to escape. Can you rescue her?

HINT: Find the huge cannon and blast the four locks from the gate to free her.

CHAPTER 3
SKY SCHOONER DOCKS

Travel with Flynn in his (relatively) safe balloon to the airship facility known as Sky Schooner Docks. If you're a fan of airships then you will find plenty of them on these islands. Much like Flynn, they are full of hot air!

OBJECTIVE
FIND THE GOLDEN PROPELLER

AREAS
GLIDER TOWER–TECH
PROPELLER FARM–UNDEAD
FORTRESS TOWER–AIR
KAW'S ISLANDS–EARTH
SHORELINE TOWER–EARTH

ITEMS TO FIND
1 SOUL GEM
1 LEGENDARY TREASURE
2 HATS
3 TREASURE CHESTS
1 STORY SCROLL

HINTS AND TIPS

GLIDER TOWER

Find the big gun and jump inside. It's time to shoot down some Drow warships!

HINT: The stripy Drow Zeppelins shoot back . . . so watch out!

PROPELLER FARM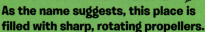

As the name suggests, this place is filled with sharp, rotating propellers.

HINT: Keep moving toward the right and use the bounce pads where possible.

FORTRESS TOWER

Here you encounter the Air Spell Punk for the first time. He casts spells on your other enemies to protect them.

HINT: Get rid of the Air Spell Punk quickly . . . Drow Spearmen aren't far behind!

KAW'S ISLANDS

If you bounce all the way to the top island you will discover a hat box containing a Jester's Hat.

HINT: Step off the top island and you will fall down to a smaller island containing a Treasure Chest.

EXTRA!

After leaving Kaw's Islands, watch out for the Goliath Drow!

SHORELINE TOWER

Here you'll find one more gun tower. Jump in, shoot down the Heavy Airship, and the propeller will be yours!

HINT: Concentrate on shooting down the largest airship. The others are an unwelcome enemy distraction.

CHAPTER 4
STORMY STRONGHOLD

Oh no! You arrive at Stormy Stronghold only to find the castle whirling around in a giant twister. Nothing's ever safe or simple in Skylands! The Drow must have discovered the Eternal Air Source and are trying to control its power.

OBJECTIVE
REBUILD THE BRIDGE
FIND THE AIR SOURCE

AREAS
THE APPROACH–LIFE
LOWER REACH–LIFE
THE BATTLEMENT–MAGIC
SKY RAMPARTS–AIR
INNER KEEP–AIR

ITEMS TO FIND
1 SOUL GEM
1 LEGENDARY TREASURE
2 HATS
3 TREASURE CHESTS
1 STORY SCROLL

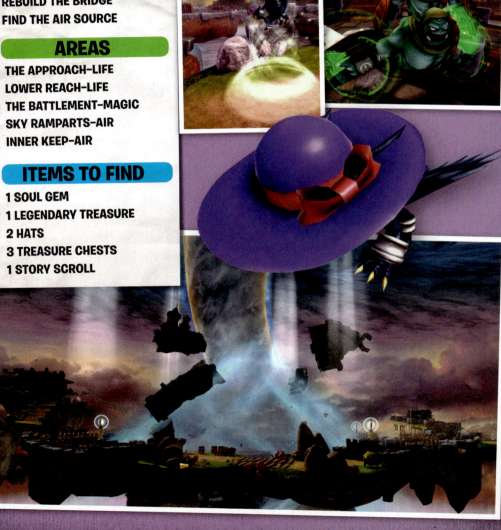

HINTS AND TIPS

THE APPROACH

Cross the second bridge and defeat an Air Spell Punk and the Drow Spearmen.

HINT: Now use a Life Skylander to get through the elemental gate.

LOWER REACH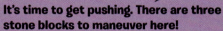

It's time to get pushing. There are three stone blocks to maneuver here!

HINT: Move the last block to reveal a teleport pad.

THE BATTLEMENT

Lower the pylon, proceed across the bridge, and move through the gate–but beware!

HINT: Once through the gate, you will battle a Drow Witch, loads of Chompies, and three Drow Spearmen!

SKY RAMPARTS

After opening the Treasure Chest it's time to move down the corridor. Watch out for those spikes!

HINT: Use the bounce pads to evade the spikes and bounce up onto a walkway to discover a bomb.

EXTRA!

Every time the bomb explodes a new one appears, so don't worry if you don't destroy the barricade on your first attempt.

INNER KEEP

Step on the floor switch to lower the gate bars and reveal access to a Soul Gem. Run to try and reach the Soul Gem before the gate rises again.

HINT: Watch the timer. It will show how much time you have left.

CHAPTER 5
OILSPILL ISLAND

Set sail and take flight to Oilspill Island with a Gillman named Gurglefin. All is not well here–trolls have captured and encaged the Gillmen and are drilling for oil to give to Kaos for his machines. You must send forth the Skylanders to set them free before they're turned into fish fingers!

OBJECTIVE

FREE THE CAGED GILLMEN
DESTROY THE TROLL REFINERY

AREAS

TADPOLE ISLAND
ACCESS PLATFORM ALPHA
SLUDGE MARSH–TECH
ACCESS PLATFORM BETA–WATER
DRILL PLATFORM DELTA–TECH
THE REFINERY–FIRE
EXHAUST VENT ZETA–TECH

ITEMS TO FIND

2 SOUL GEMS
1 LEGENDARY TREASURE
1 HAT
3 TREASURE CHESTS
1 STORY SCROLL

HINTS AND TIPS

EXTRA!
After you go up the ramp, bounce to the left to find a Treasure Chest.

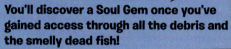

ACCESS PLATFORM ALPHA
Look out! You're about to come face to face with the first Troll Greasemonkey.

HINT: Stand back so as not to get struck. Try to defeat them from a distance!

SLUDGE MARSH
You'll discover a Soul Gem once you've gained access through all the debris and the smelly dead fish!

HINT: If you have Wham-Shell you'll be able to use this Soul Gem to unlock his Carapace Plating power.

EXTRA!
Watch out for Troll Grenadier overhead!

DRILL PLATFORM DELTA
There's an awful lot to do in this area—redirect energy beams, find a key, free a prisoner, and defeat a new foe.

HINT: Look out for the Troll Grenadier's assault from above as you rotate the laser beam.

THE REFINERY
The Refinery is made up of a load of pipes that connects lots of different platforms.

HINT: Be careful not to get lost. It's easy to lose your way in this pipe maze.

EXHAUST VENT ZETA
Gurglefin will encourage you to ascend the final ramp that will lead you to the Exhaust Vent Zeta.

HINT: Throw in the ticking bomb to destroy the Refinery and save the Gillmen.

CHAPTER 6
DARK WATER COVE

Gurglefin takes you on a further adventure. This time you venture to a nasty and eerie place called Dark Water Cove. You must first find the location of the Twin Spouts. However, this is not as easy as it would appear. The main gates are closed, so you must find a way inside.

OBJECTIVE

LOCATE THE TWIN SPOUTS
RETRIEVE THE TWIN SPOUTS
ESCAPE IN THE PIRATE SHIP

AREAS

THE NORTH STAR
BATTERY ISLAND-EARTH
WHALE'S BELLY
EAST GATE-WATER
LOST RIGGER'S COVE-MAGIC
TORTA'S TOWN-EARTH
BRIDGE OF HANDS
THE ANCIENT TEMPLE-MAGIC
THE ELVENSHIP-WATER
WEST GATE
WATERY GRAVES-WATER

ITEMS TO FIND

2 SOUL GEMS
1 LEGENDARY TREASURE
2 HATS
3 TREASURE CHESTS
1 STORY SCROLL

HINTS AND TIPS

EXTRA! Don't get too attached to Gurglefin's ship–it might not be around for long!

📖 THE NORTH STAR

Board the North Star pirate ship and find the Soul Gem on board for Dino-Rang's Sticky Boomerangs.

HINT: Whatever you do, keep out of the chrosshairs of the local artillery!

BATTERY ISLAND 🔖

Destroy the stone wall, but look out! Beyond the wall is a Nauteloid.

HINT: Nauteloids charge at you pretty quickly. Make sure you get them before they get you!

📖 LOST RIGGER'S COVE

Once you've defeated the Blastaneers, use the bounce pads to reach a Lock Puzzle.

HINT: Make sure you find the tiki hat in the hat box. this will boost your elemental powers.

THE ANCIENT TEMPLE 🔖

It's an ambush! As soon as you enter the temple you're trapped. Defeat the enemy and cross the bridge.

HINT: Wipe out more foes and you'll find the Twin Spouts!

📖 WATERY GRAVES

Move from one raft to the next to move down the river until you find the rafts with the bounce pads.

HINT: Once you've moved across all the rafts you'll discover the Tropical Turban hat box.

CHAPTER 7
LEViATHAN LAGOON

Team up with Gurglefin once more and set sail for this dangerous lagoon. You must discover the four statues and place them in the Shrine to reveal the Water Source. But watch out . . . you're not the only one who wants the statues!

OBJECTIVE

BRING FOUR STATUES TO THE SHRINE

FIND THE WATER SOURCE

AREAS

PEARL CLUSTER

PLANK WALK–WATER

TURTLE ISLAND–LIFE

SHARK'S TOOTH ISLAND–WATER

THE SHRINE–MAGIC

ITEMS TO FIND

1 SOUL GEM

1 LEGENDARY TREASURE

1 HAT

3 TREASURE CHESTS

1 STORY SCROLL

HINTS AND TIPS

EXTRA!

Watch out for the overturned boats. Nauteloids hide underneath!

PEARL CLUSTER

Cross the first two bridges to discover the first of the four statues.

HINT: A Hob 'n' Yaro has gotten there first. Destroy it to recover the statue.

PLANK WALK

Enter the Water Elemental Gate and cross the wooden bridge to reach the three islands.

HINT: Whatever you do, don't use the teleport pad. It'll send you back to the start! You don't want that!

TURTLE ISLAND

You'll reach Turtle Island by walking along the chain walkways.

HINT: When you reach the three turtles, push them into the gap to form a bridge. Watch out for another Hob 'n' Yaro here!

SHARK'S TOOTH ISLAND

Find a "Love for the Sea" Soul Gem here. It can be used with Zap.

HINT: You'll find another statue here, but a Hob 'n' Yaro has gotten there first—again!

THE SHRINE

Place all four statues around the Shrine to reveal the Water Element.

HINT: Watch out! As soon as you've done this you'll be gobbled by the Leviathan . . . and come face to face with Kaos.

CHAPTER 8
CRYSTAL EYE CASTLE

Crystal Eye Castle is a dangerous fortress. There are two Seeing Towers that will have to be destroyed to open the big gate. You will be greeted by a friendly mole called Diggs who had his eyesight restored by the magical powers of the Crystal Eye.

OBJECTIVE

DESTROY THE TWO TOWERS
GET THE CRYSTAL EYE

AREAS

THE GAUNTLET–EARTH
OUTER COURTYARD–AIR
PUZZLE PIT–EARTH
SECRET TOWER–UNDEAD
EAST TOWER–TECH
INNER COURTYARD
WEST TOWER–TECH
THE TOWER OF EYES–AIR

ITEMS TO FIND

1 SOUL GEM
1 LEGENDARY TREASURE
2 HATS
3 TREASURE CHESTS
1 STORY SCROLL

HINTS AND TIPS

📖 THE GAUNTLET

The moment you enter the castle a pair of one-eyed Timidclops start rolling explosive barrels in your direction.

HINT: Weave around the rolling barrels or destroy them as you head up the slope.

OUTER COURTYARD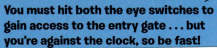

You must hit both the eye switches to gain access to the entry gate . . . but you're against the clock, so be fast!

HINT: Travel up the stairs to the left of the Cyclops Cruncher to discover a Story Scroll from Professor P. Grungally.

📖 EAST TOWER

Look out! Through the doors is the mighty Cyclops Mammoth! There's an awful lot of one-eyed beasts around here!

HINT: You might destroy the Cyclops Mammoth easily, but watch out for those nipping Chompies!

WEST TOWER 👉

The West Tower doors will automatically let you in. Watch out for the Cyclops Chuckers!

HINT: Try destroying the podiums that hold the Chuckers as you can't attack the Chuckers themselves.

📖 THE TOWER OF EYES

Whether Cyclops Chuckers or Cyclops Choppers, they're all here to get you. Keep an eye on them . . . they certainly have one on you!

HINT: You must defeat all the enemies here to lower the spear gate and retrieve the Crystal Eye.

CHAPTER 9
STONETOWN

It's digging time! You'll meet up with Diggs again and he'll lead you over the stone bridge to a Cyclops outpost. This is as far as the mole can take you, so you're on your own from here. But look out–you're on shaky ground!

OBJECTIVE

DEFEAT THE STONE GOLEM

AREAS

MUSHROOM RIDGE-LIFE
OLD CYCLOPS FORT-LIFE
BLUE WATER SWAMP-WATER
NEW FORTRESS-EARTH
TOWN OUTSKIRTS
WAYWARD TOWN-LIFE
RUMBLING RAVINE

ITEMS TO FIND

2 SOUL GEMS
1 LEGENDARY TREASURE
1 HAT
3 TREASURE CHESTS
1 STORY SCROLL

HINTS AND TIPS

MUSHROOM RIDGE

You must gain access to the Cyclops outpost through the gate. Destroy those ever-familiar Chompies first, though!

HINT: Press both eye switches to open the gate and sprint through.

OLD CYCLOPS FORT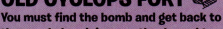

You must find the bomb and get back to the purple bomb icon on the ground to explode the boulder-ridden entrance.

HINT: Inside the cave you'll find the Legendary Treasure named MONo LISA. Keep an eye out for it . . . it has an eye out for you!

BLUE WATER SWAMP

It's turtle-pushing time! You'll need to form a bridge to get across the water. What better way than to use the turtles?

HINT: Watch out for the blowfish-hurling Squiddlers! Those annoying things!

NEW FORTRESS

There are four stone blocks that you must maneuver once inside. Do this correctly and you'll gain access to a platform containing a key.

HINT: A Hob 'n' Yaro has one of the keys. This one's a pain to catch!

TOWN OUTSKIRTS

There's a Life Elemental Gate in this area. To find it, cross the bridge and head to the left.

HINT: A Treasure Chest awaits you once you pass through the Life Gate into Wayward Town.

CHAPTER 10
TREETOP TERRACE

It's all the way to the top for you as you ride the giant vine to Treetop Terrace. However, the Drow have gotten there first. They have stolen the Life Seeds. You must track down the Life Seeds in order to find the Eternal Life Source.

OBJECTIVE
COLLECT THE LIFE SEEDS

AREAS
THE CANOPY-AIR
THE SLUICE GATE-LIFE
THE HOLLOW-LIFE
ANCIENT TRUNK-MAGIC
THE SEED TREE-LIFE

ITEMS TO FIND
1 SOUL GEM
1 LEGENDARY TREASURE
1 HAT
3 TREASURE CHESTS
1 STORY SCROLL

HINTS AND TIPS

THE CANOPY
Here be giant hornets. And this really *is* a giant one! Look out for this stunning Corn Hornet who's in no mood to play.

HINT: Don't let it get too close. That sting is not for decoration!

THE SLUICE GATE
There are rolling barrels here that will detonate when they reach the bottom of the slope. Boom!

HINT: Make sure you get the Treasure Chest to the right before attacking the slope.

THE HOLLOW
Teleport to The Hollow, where you'll come face to face with a Blitzer Bully. Turn the handle and move through the opening on the right.

HINT: You'll find a teleport pad through there to take you back.

ANCIENT TRUNK
Through the Magic Elemental Gate you'll find an Anchor Cannon Soul Gem for Gill Grunt.

HINT: Beyond the teleport pad is bounce pad paradise . . . and a Moose Hat!

THE SEED TREE
There's plenty of minions and guards here to try and stop you from getting the Life Seeds.

HINT: Destroy all the enemies to free the Life Seeds. Good job!

CHAPTER 11
FALLING FOREST

The Eternal Life Source presents itself in the form of an acorn. Kaos is getting his Lumberjack Trolls to cut down every tree to try to find it. It is your job to find it before our ever-present evil Portal Master and his trolls do.

OBJECTIVE

FIND THE LIFE SOURCE

AREAS

OWL'S ROOST–TECH
PINECONE'S LANDING–LIFE
THE ACORN STASH–EARTH
THE GREAT STUMP–EARTH

ITEMS TO FIND

1 SOUL GEM
1 LEGENDARY TREASURE
1 HAT
3 TREASURE CHESTS
1 STORY SCROLL

HINTS AND TIPS

⬅ OWL'S ROOST

First thing's first: Let's start to destroy those ghastly tree-chopping machines. Kaos can't get away with this!

HINT: On your way down the wooden platform, stop and collect the rockets.

EXTRA!

This area contains the Sylvan Regeneration Soul Gem for Stealth Elf.

PINECONE'S LANDING ➡

Destroy the trolls in front of the chainsaw tank and then take out the tank itself.

HINT: There's a Tech Spell Punk to eliminate before you continue.

Moves: 0   0 / 6 u

⬅ THE ACORN STASH

There are two Troll Grenadiers on a raised balcony. Up there with them is a Treasure Chest. The only way to get up there is via the teleport pad.

HINT: You must solve a lock puzzle to reach the teleport pad and reach the platform.

THE GREAT STUMP ➡

Kaos is back. Here comes the Dark Missile—the first of Kaos' military minions to attack. It spawns a collection of tough mushrooms as a shield.

HINT: You can eliminate the mushrooms with constant attacks, or just run around them—whatever works!

CHAPTER 12
TROLL WAREHOUSE

You enter the Troll Warehouse via the access elevator, lead by Secret Agent Snuckles. Remember him? You saved him earlier when a tornado ripped through his village. He's since joined the Mabu Defense Force and . . . well, it doesn't really matter. It's time to get to work!

OBJECTIVE

FIND THE TROLL WAREHOUSE
FIND THE PIECES OF THE MAP
GET THROUGH THE MINEFIELD

AREAS

RESEARCH BASE OMEGA–LIFE
THE FOUNDRY–LIFE
THE MINEFIELD–LIFE
ISOLATION CELLS–LIFE
ACCESS CATWALKS–TECH
LAVA REFUGE–FIRE
WAREHOUSE 14

ITEMS TO FIND

1 SOUL GEM
1 LEGENDARY TREASURE
2 HATS
3 TREASURE CHESTS
1 STORY SCROLL

HINTS AND TIPS

RESEARCH BASE OMEGA
Here's where you start, but you won't get far without solving a Lock Puzzle.

HINT: Roll over the three glowing circles to solve the puzzle.

EXTRA!

Keep your eyes open for the MIRV Mortar Soul Gem for Zook.

THE WORKSHOP
As soon as you descend the ramp you'll come face to face with a Trollverine.

HINT: His balance is way off! When he loses control it's time to strike!

ISOLATION CELLS
There's a Treasure Chest, a Hat box and a Legendary Item in this area. You'll need a Life Skylander to enter.

HINT: to collect all the items, complete the puzzle lock door instead of a locked gate.

ACCESS CATWALKS
Get the Treasure Chest, destroy the wooden gate, and climb the stairs to reach the last puzzle piece.

HINT: Heading this way will lead you to a Fire Elemental Gate.

WAREHOUSE 14
Having completed the Minefield Map, you can now head across to this area more safely.

HINT: Sit back and watch the rocket launch into the blue sky. Well done!

CHAPTER 13
GOO FACTORY

Having collected the Golden Gear at the Troll Warehouse, you must now find the special grease that will make it work– Green Primordial Goo! You must shut down the troll's Goo Factory and recover the green goo before the Troll Military uses it for themselves.

OBJECTIVE

FIND THE MABU CAPTAIN
LEVEL THE WALL WITH A MEGA BOMB
RAISE ALL GOO FACTORY FLAGS

AREAS

WESTERN TRENCHES–EARTH
SANDBAG HILL–EARTH
POTATO FARM–AIR
THE AMMO DUMP–TECH
TWENTY STONE DEFENSE–FIRE

ITEMS TO FIND

1 SOUL GEM
1 LEGENDARY TREASURE
2 HATS
3 TREASURE CHESTS
1 STORY SCROLL

HINTS AND TIPS

WESTERN TRENCHES

It's tough in the trenches and plenty of familiar enemies await.

HINT: Immediately head up the ramp on the left to get the reusable bomb. Hurl bombs into the trenches to destroy some hostile foes.

SANDBAG HILL

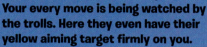

Your every move is being watched by the trolls. Here they even have their yellow aiming target firmly on you.

HINT: Don't step in the target when it turns red. It means they're about to fire.

POTATO FARM

On the wooden platform you will discover a Legendary Treasure, guarded by a Rocket Imp and an Earth Spell Punk.

HINT: Use the Teleport pad to instantly get back across the field safely.

THE AMMO DUMP

It's time to follow your friend Nort. He has discovered a secret way into the Ammo Dump.

HINT: After leaving Nort, find the Mega Bomb to gain entry.

EXTRA!
In the Ammo Dump there's an Orbiting Sun Shield Soul Gem for Camo and a Treasure Chest.

TWENTY STONE DEFENSE

On the far side of the boxes is a Treasure Chest and a Hat box.

HINT: Push the boxes into the right positions to gain access to the goodies!

145

CHAPTER 14
BATTLEFIELD

The situation is not good. The trolls have overrun the Mabu defenses and cut off the Command Team. It's time to help those poor Mabu once more. Try to reach their Command Team as quickly as you can.

OBJECTIVE

FIND THE COMMAND TEAM
GET TECH SOURCE FROM FORT

AREAS

SOUTHERN TRENCHES-TECH
THE BIRD'S NEST
DEFENSIVE PERIMETER-FIRE
NO MAN'S LAND-UNDEAD
THE STADIUM-UNDEAD
TECH BASE THETA-UNDEAD

ITEMS TO FIND

2 SOUL GEMS
1 LEGENDARY TREASURE
1 HAT
3 TREASURE CHESTS
1 STORY SCROLL

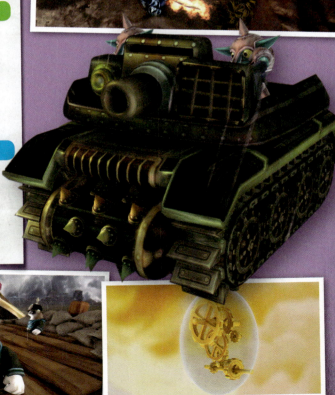

HINTS AND TIPS

EXTRA!

Firing the cannon will reveal a Legendary Treasure and a Treasure Chest in the far-off field. You can collect these later.

SOUTHERN TRENCHES

Head to the right to find the bomb and bring it back to the purple bomb icon. This will destroy the barricade in front of you.

HINT: Head up the slope into The Bird's Nest and fire the cannon.

DEFENSIVE PERIMETER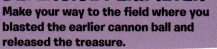

Make your way to the field where you blasted the earlier cannon ball and released the treasure.

HINT: Watch out! Land mines are littered all around. Tread carefully to retrieve the treasure and head back to the Southern Trenches.

NO MAN'S LAND

Cross the bone bridge into this zone using an Undead Skylander. You'll need a Mega Bomb to blow up the wall here.

HINT: Use the teleport pad to reach the basement. demolish the wall to find the Mega Bomb.

THE STADIUM

You've just unleashed the trolls' colossal tank, powered by the Eternal Tech Source! Oh no! How will you destroy this manic machine?

HINT: You must collect Mega Bombs from Tech Base Theta to destroy the Trolls' mega machine.

TECH BASE THETA

You must destroy the Troll Turret as it constantly fires at you. Then, unleash your fury on the mega troll tank by using the reusable bombs.

HINT: There's a Treasure Chest at the top of the ramp. Don't miss it!

CHAPTER 15
CRAWLING CATACOMBS

It's time to descend into the Crawling Catacombs. Sounds scary, doesn't it? That's because it is! Don't worry, though. You'll soon have a skeleton guide named T-Bone to show you around. That is, until he runs away in fear before you even get started!

OBJECTIVE
FIND THE SKULL MASK

AREAS
PIT OF WEBS–UNDEAD
ALCHEMY LAB–UNDEAD
CHAMBER OF EYES–UNDEAD
THE SKITTERING DARK–FIRE
THE WIDOW'S COURT–MAGIC

ITEMS TO FIND
1 SOUL GEM
1 LEGENDARY TREASURE
1 HAT
3 TREASURE CHESTS
1 STORY SCROLL

HINTS AND TIPS

 ## PIT OF WEBS

It's arachnid central in here! Once you enter you'll be set upon by Spider Swarmers. Look out!

HINT: Kill off these new enemies before they attack you and explode into a dangerous green cloud.

ALCHEMY LAB

Check out the Story Scroll in the Alchemy Lab as well as the treasure.

HINT: This story Scroll tells you about me, Master Eon, and my early days before I became a Portal Master.

EXTRA!

Watch out for the Fat Belly Spiders who leave a pool of goo and the Spider Spitters who, er, spit spiders!

THE CHAMBER OF EYES

There's a hat box hidden in one of the chambers. Blast into the first chamber and work your way through each one, pressing the eye switches as you go.

HINT: Avoid the rotating blades and deadly spears at all costs!

THE SKITTERING DARK

Find two keys to unlock the gate to Widow's Court. Your vision is restricted so be alert!

HINT: Watch out for the Fat Belly Spiders, Gargantula guard, Moon Widows, and Spider Spitters!

WIDOW'S COURT

Your mission in here is to try to grab that elusive Skull Mask behind the spear gate.

HINT: Destroy the spiders and steer clear of their webs! The spear gate will only open once the last spider is destroyed.

CHAPTER 16
CADAVEROUS CRYPT

Now it's off to find the Skeleton Key. It's kept somewhere in this dark and spooky crypt. Some of the creatures down here haven't seen outside life in centuries. But if you think they're glad to see you then think again!

OBJECTIVE

FIND THE SKELETON KEY

AREAS

THE CATACOMBS–FIRE
THE EVERSHIFTING HALL–UNDEAD
MAZE OF SKULLS–TECH
THE SHRINE OF THE UNLIVING–UNDEAD

ITEMS TO FIND

2 SOUL GEMS
1 LEGENDARY TREASURE
2 HATS
3 TREASURE CHESTS
1 STORY SCROLL

HINTS AND TIPS

Look out for the Rotting Robbies. They are easily destroyed with fire and cannon balls.

THE EVERSHIFTING HALL

As you enter the Evershifting Hall, the gate will shut behind you. This stops any unwanted Rhu-Barbs and Undead Spell Punks from pursuing you.

HINT: Fight off the Rhu-Babies and move down the following two sets of stairs.

MAZE OF SKULLS

Reach the Maze of Skulls by using a Tech Skylander to unlock the gate and move across the bridge. Find the teleport pad and this will take you into an area where you will be given a Heroic Challenge to collect ten Enchanted Skulls.

HINT: You have limited time, so make sure you have a plan and get moving!

EXTRA!

Finding all ten skulls in time will present your Skylander with a hat box. This box contains the Crown of Light.

THE SHRINE OF THE UNLIVING

You'll find the Skeleton Key in here. The only way to get through the doors and retrieve it is to destroy all the enemies first.

HINT: Make sure you are using an Undead Skylander in here. You'll need all the extra strength and power you can get to defeat the onslaught of enemies.

CHAPTER 17
CREEPY CITADEL

This is where the Eternal Undead Source rests in peace! After descending the staircase, T-Bone lets you through the gate. Most people would find it hard to enter, but luckily T-Bone uses his head . . . literally!

OBJECTIVE

ENTER THE CASTLE
COLLECT THE UNDEAD SOURCE

AREAS

SKELETON GATE–WATER
TOMB OF STONES–AIR
MAIN GATE–UNDEAD
BOX GOBLIN SWAMP–WATER
THE GALLERY–UNDEAD
THE GRAND BALLROOM–UNDEAD
THE UNDEAD GATEWAY - UNDEAD

ITEMS TO FIND

1 SOUL GEM
1 LEGENDARY TREASURE
1 HAT
3 TREASURE CHESTS
1 STORY SCROLL

HINTS AND TIPS

EXTRA!

Solve the crystal puzzle at Skeleton Gate and it will end up opening a drawbridge.

SKELETON GATE

As you pass through the gate you'll discover a Story Scroll. After that, go in search of the crystal puzzle.

HINT: push one of the crystals and keep pulling the switch until the beam deflects in the correct place.

BOX GOBLIN SWAMP

These goblins won't hurt you but they're pretty stubborn. They don't plan to move to let you through.

HINT: One of the floor switches is pretty big. You'll need to push the block over it to help.

THE GALLERY

Move along the corridor-being careful to avoid the axe blades that swing from the walls on either side.

HINT: When confronted by Shadow Knights, it'll take a lot of power to defeat them.

THE GRAND BALLROOM

It's time to solve another puzzle. This is a block puzzle that will open the exit gate when completed.

HINT: Stand on the floor buttons and keep a sharp look out for the decapitating blades!

THE UNDEAD GATEWAY

Step into the circle to be transported to a battle area. Come face to face with Kaos and some of his nastiest minions!

HINT: Make sure you have plenty of healthy Skylanders at your disposal. This battle is a toughie.

CHAPTER 18
MOLEKIN MINE

It's time for a reunion! Remember Blobbers, who you saved back on Shattered Island? No!? Well, he remembers you. Anyway, he's trapped in the mine along with some Molekin Miners. Guess who needs to save them all? That's right! A Skylander's heroic work is never done.

OBJECTIVE

RESCUE ALL 7 MOLEKIN MINERS
PUSH DIGGS TO SAFETY

AREAS

ACCESS TUNNEL VIN-EARTH
THE SECRET CLAIM-TECH
THE UNDERGROUND LAKE-WATER
THE CRYSTAL GROVE-WATER

ITEMS TO FIND

2 SOUL GEMS
1 LEGENDARY TREASURE
1 HAT
3 TREASURE CHESTS
1 STORY SCROLL

HINTS AND TIPS

ACCESS TUNNEL VIN

Go and save the first miner! This miner is accompanied by Flame Imps. Destroy them and make your first rescue before continuing down the tunnel.

HINT: In between firing molten lava balls the rock monster stops shooting. This is the time to get attacking and bring him down!

THE SECRET CLAIM

Enter through the gate and smash through the rocks with the miner's pick. On the other side you'll discover a cannon. There's a hat box beyond the stone blocks and the crystals.

HINT: Move the blocks, fire the cannon to smash the crystals, and retrieve the hat box containing a Miner Hat!

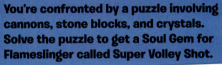

EXTRA!

You'll discover a Story Scroll next to the miner in The Underground Lake. Read it to see who created the Core of Light.

THE UNDERGROUND LAKE

There's plenty of fire in this mine, and the fire's about to get even stronger! Watch out for the Lava King. He is hotheaded and burning with a desire to destroy you.

HINT: Smash through the next three piles of rubble to find and rescue another Molekin Miner.

THE CRYSTAL GROVE

You're confronted by a puzzle involving cannons, stone blocks, and crystals. Solve the puzzle to get a Soul Gem for Flameslinger called Super Volley Shot.

HINT: Once you've collected the Soul Gem, push the Molekin into the mining cart. He's protecting the Crucible that's also in the cart. Get them to Blobbers and your task is complete.

CHAPTER 19
LAVA LAKEs RAILWAY

Join Diggs and hop on the superfast train to the Underground Caves in search of the Eternal Fire Source. But be warned, this is no joy ride. The Underground Caves are filled with deep-dwelling creatures, so have your strongest Skylanders at the ready.

OBJECTIVE

USE THE TRACK SWITCHES
REPAIR THE TRAIN TRACKS
FIND THE FIRE SOURCE

AREAS

THE MOLEKIN MINES–UNDEAD
CRYSTAL GROTTOS–UNDEAD
LAVA LAGOON–FIRE
FIREY DEPTHS–FIRE
THE FIRE SOURCE

ITEMS TO FIND

1 SOUL GEM
1 LEGENDARY TREASURE
1 HAT
3 TREASURE CHESTS
1 STORY SCROLL

HINTS AND TIPS

THE MOLEKIN MINES

Once you leave the relative safety of the train you'll be greeted by a rather unpleasant Fire Spell Punk.

HINT: Watch out for the Fire Spell Punk barrels—they're rather explosive!

CRYSTAL GROTTOS

Find the lever to open the gate to the Crystal Grottos.

HINT: Once inside you'll need to help Diggs repair the path for the train. Push the stone blocks to fill the gap so he can build a track on top.

LAVA LAGOON

Lava Lagoon is exactly what it sounds like. Ready for the challenge? Things are about to heat up!

HINT: Take a good look down at Lava Lagoon before you continue.

FIERY DEPTHS

Enter this area through the Eternal Fire Gate where you'll find a hat box containing the Lil Devil Hat.

HINT: If you use a Fire Skylander they can walk on the lava!

THE FIRE SOURCE

Defeat Kaos' Dark Pyro Archer, Dark Phoenix Dragon, and Dark Evil Eruptor to win the Eternal Fire Source from Kaos.

HINT: Once you've defeated them all, they'll come back one more time, so be ready!

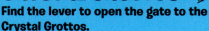

157

CHAPTER 20
QUICKSILVER VAULT

Meet the Weapon Master who will explain all about the final Eternal Source you require–Magic. You will need to find a very special, ancient oil. This will allow every other Element to receive the magic and is vital to restoring the Core of Light.

OBJECTIVE

UNLOCK THE GATE TO THE VAULT
ACTIVATE THE VAULT BEAMS
FIND THE QUICKSILVER VAULT

AREAS

SKELETON GATE–AIR
MAIN GATE–AIR
DIMENSIONAL RIFTS–LIFE
THE SCION OF EARTH–MAGIC
THE GRAND BALLROOM–MAGIC

ITEMS TO FIND

1 SOUL GEM
1 LEGENDARY TREASURE
1 HAT
3 TREASURE CHESTS
1 STORY SCROLL

HINTS AND TIPS

SKELETON GATE

Prepare to do battle with some ancient Arkeyan weaponry as you come across Blasters guarding the gate.

HINT: Don't move into the electric charges thrown out by the Arkeyan Blasters. It won't do you any good!

MAIN GATE

Arrive at the Main Gate via a teleport pad where a confrontation with a Magic Spell Punk awaits you.

HINT: This foe creates reanimated Magic balls to attack you. Destroy the Magic Spell Punk before it creates too many!

DIMENSIONAL RIFTS

Teleport to a collection of four floating islands that yield a hat box and Legendary Treasure.

HINT: The only way to get to each island is via the moving stone blocks.

THE SCION OF EARTH

Align the three energy beams with the three seals to open the Quicksilver Vault.

HINT: Watch out for the Arkeyan Ultrons on the way.

CHAPTER 21
ARKEYAN ARMORY

The Eternal Magic Source is locked away in the caverns of the Arkeyan Armory. You are in for a real treat as you are about to witness, firsthand, the expanse of the Arkeyan civilisation and its immense power.

OBJECTIVE

USE ROBOT TO FIND TEMPLE
USE SECURITY CARD ON PANEL
FIND THE MAGIC SOURCE

AREAS

UNYIELDING GARRISON-TECH
HALLS OF MOLTEN FIRE
THE CRUCIBLE-AIR
PANDORAN GIFT SHOP-AIR
THE VAULT

ITEMS TO FIND

1 SOUL GEM
1 LEGENDARY TREASURE
1 HAT
3 TREASURE CHESTS
1 STORY SCROLL

HINTS AND TIPS

UNYIELDING GARRISON

Restore light to the cave and reveal the Arkeyan war machines.

HINT: Be careful of the Defense Drones. The only way to destroy them is to disintegrate their Control Towers.

HALLS OF MOLTEN FIRE

It's Defense Drone central in here! They are relentless as you move through the tunnel. Oh, by the way, there are Arkeyan Ultrons in here too!

HINT: As you are now piloting a War Machine, these foes will do you little damage.

THE CRUCIBLE

In order to unlock the Main Vault and release the Eternal Magic Source, you will need a security key card.

HINT: The security key card can be found on the lower level of the temple.

PANDORAN GIFT SHOP

Access this area through the Air Elemental Gate and then via the whirlwind beyond. Use the boxes to ride between the platforms.

HINT: If you fall off, just head for the teleport pad to get back to the top.

 ### THE VAULT

On finding the security card, take it back to the Security Control Panel.

HINT: You must now deactivate the three switches. Each one is inside a vault.

CHAPTER 22
LAIR OF KAOS

Are you prepared to enter the portal to the flying thorn fortress that is known as the Lair of Kaos? I hope so. This is where all your hard work has brought you, my young Portal Master. The Core of Light is restored and you must now undertake your final and most difficult challenge. Good luck, and watch out for those metallic claws!

OBJECTIVE
FIND ENTRANCE TO THE CASTLE

AREAS
COLDFIRE CRATER–FIRE
PATH OF FANGS–MAGIC
ALTERNATE ENDS
TOWERS OF DARKNESS–FIRE
FORLORN ISLANDS–MAGIC
THE FARTHEST REACH–EARTH

ITEMS TO FIND
1 SOUL GEM
1 LEGENDARY TREASURE
1 HAT
3 TREASURE CHESTS
1 STORY SCROLL

HINTS AND TIPS

COLDFIRE CRATER

Dispose of the Fire Imps and move to the teleport pad. This will transport you to a platform with a locked gate.

HINT: To reach the key you'll have to face a Lava King and Drow Witches. Destroy them quickly!

PATH OF FANGS

The entrance to this area is exactly as it sounds–so don't be shocked!

EXTRA!

Through the Magic Elemental Gate you'll find a hat box containing Wabbit Ears.

HINT: These fangs will try to electrify you, so be careful how you step.

TOWERS OF DARKNESS

You'll find a gate that needs three keys to open it. The first key is here in Towers of Darkness.

HINT: Once you've found the first key, move up the right fork to search for the second.

FORLORN ISLANDS

You've done incredibly well to get this far, but don't drop your guard. Drow Witches and Shadow Knights are waiting for you.

HINT: Be sure to explore this area fully, or you may miss out on a treasure chest.

THE FINAL CHALLENGE: PREPARE TO MEET KAOS

After collecting all three keys and opening the gate, you'll gain access to Kaos' castle.

Here you'll come face to face with the evil Portal Master and every minion he can throw at you.

HINT: Be prepared—this onslaught is relentless!

ADVENTURE
Packs

PIRATE SEAS

The Pirate Seas bonus map is packed with swashbuckling adventure. You'll have a ball in this section . . . a cannonball that is!

SKYLANDER IN PACK
TERRAFIN

EXTRAS
PIRATE SEAS BONUS MAP
PIRATE COVE BATTLE MODE ARENA

MAGIC ITEMS

Ghost Swords

Hidden Treasure

DARKLIGHT CRYPT

This area is not for the fainthearted. It is strong with the undead and filled with skulduggery at every turn!

SKYLANDER IN PACK
GHOST ROASTER

EXTRAS
DARKLIGHT CRYPT BONUS MAP
THE NECROPOLIS BATTLE MODE ARENA

MAGIC ITEMS

Healing Elixir

Time Twister

EMPIRE OF ICE

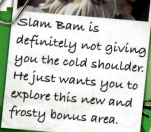

Slam Bam is definitely not giving you the cold shoulder. He just wants you to explore this new and frosty bonus area.

SKYLANDER IN PACK
SLAM BAM

EXTRAS
EMPIRE OF ICE BONUS MAP
ICICLE ISLE BATTLE MODE ARENA

MAGIC ITEMS

Anvil Rain

Sky-Iron Shield

DRAGON'S PEAK

Fang goodness for Sunburn! He has the ability to lead you into Dragon's Peak to seek adventure. Look around and . . . well, have a peek!

SKYLANDER IN PACK
SUNBURN

EXTRAS
DRAGON'S PEAK BONUS MAP
CUBE DUNGEON BATTLE MODE ARENA

MAGIC ITEMS

Sparx Dragonfly

Winged Boots

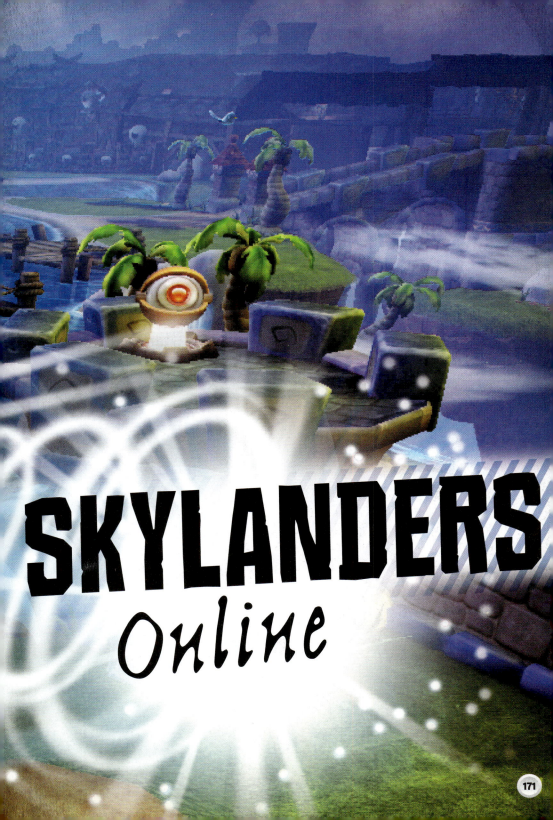

SKYLANDERS
Online

WELCOME TO THE WEBSITE

ENTERING THE SITE

If you're eager to embark upon a new Skylands adventure or want to play with other budding Portal Masters who love Skylanders as much as you do, you should head for the Skylanders Spyro's Universe™ website (universe. skylanders.com).

Here, you can play games with your favorite characters, build a Skyland of your very own, chat with other players, and even try out Skylanders you do not yet own!

THERE ARE LOTS OF WAYS TO PLAY IN SKYLANDERS SPYRO'S UNIVERSE!

PLAY NOW

It takes just three easy steps to register an account and start playing! From there, you can immediately jump into the action. You don't even need a toy to play . . . but you'll have access to new games and abilities if you do!

PLAY GAMES

The online world is packed full of games and activities. You can fling sheep, fight bad guys, shoot cannons, smash castles, and much more! You can also show off your in-game rewards to your friends.

YOUR SKYLAND

Look upon your own personal Skyland as a place for you to express yourself. You can show off your collection of Skylanders, play additional games, and use your in-game currency to make it look however you'd like. Check it out!

COMMUNITY AND BLOGS

Keep your Portal Master eyes peeled for updates to our blog, along with other additions to the rapidly expanding Skylanders Spyro's Universe!

GAME FEATURES

Learn all about the features of the Skylanders game– including how you can take your Skylanders to a friend's house to continue your adventure together.

PLAY WITH YOUR FRIENDS

Skylanders Spyro's Universe is an online multiplayer game where Portal Masters from all over the world can play together. You can play games, help your friends, and even have a dance off!

EXPAND YOUR ADVENTURE

Just because you've finished the console game, it doesn't mean your adventure is over. Skylanders Spyro's Universe lets you use all your toys in a massive multiplayer game. A whole new universe of possibilities awaits!

EXCLUSIVE PENGUIN!

To thank you for reading my guide to the wonders of Skylands, I have prepared a very special gift for you. A number of penguins roam the landscape of Skylanders Spyro's Universe, and I have arranged for one to accompany you on your journey. To have him join you on your Skyland, simply follow these steps . . .

Create an account at universe.skylanders.com.

From the customization menu, choose "I have a code."

Enter the following code, and you will now have a penguin all your own!

PENGUIN

(You'll need a mirror to see it!)

ONLINE SAFETY

FOR **KIDS**

At Skylanders Spyro's Universe you can play games, read blogs, learn about new game features, and leave comments to let us know what you think. Here are some tips to make sure you're always safe online.

Never give out your personal information, such as your real name, address, or phone number. Keep your web-code card numbers safe and secret so no one else can register your Skylanders online!

FOR **PARENTS**

Our primary goal at Skylanders Spyro's Universe is to provide an online virtual world that allows your children to creatively express themselves and interact with other children within a safe environment. All of the chats in Skylanders Spyro's Universe consist of prewritten and approved phrases that are selected by your child. The phrases have been written with the goal of promoting fun interactions that still allow your children to be creative in their expressions. By using preapproved phrases, at no point will any child be allowed to type in their own content or share any personal information with any other users. In addition, the site has active staff members who monitor daily game play to ensure safety.